The
Cat
Handbook

Karen Leigh Davis

BARRON'S

A Word About Pronouns

Many cat lovers feel that the pronoun "it" is not appropriate when referring to a beloved pet. For this reason, cats are referred to as "he" throughout this book unless the topic specifically relates to female cats. No gender bias is intended by this writing style.

About the Author

Karen Leigh Davis has a background in journalism and business writing. She has written a pet care column and numerous books and feature articles on cats and other companion animals for national and regional magazines and newspapers. As a freelance writer with more than 25 years of experience, she has conducted extensive research on animal-related topics with veterinarians, breeders, and other experts. Davis comes from a cat-loving family and has a lifetime of experience living in the company of cats. A former breeder and cat show exhibitor, she finds all felines, purebred or mixed, domestic or wild, irresistibly charming and beautiful. She lives in Roanoke, VIrginia, with four cats.

Photo Credits

Joan Balzarini: pages 23, 35, 38, 43, 46, 47, 49, 66, 77, 78, 80, 81, 90, 96, 103, 104, 107, 109, 111, 124, 129, 137, 161, 165, 183; Norvia Behling: pages 19, 39, 126, 172, 175, 190; Seth Casteel: pages 65, 95, 117, 149, 153, 186, 187; Kent Dannen: pages 14, 27, 48, 50, 52, 97, 99, 100, 115, 151; Shirley Fernandez: pages 61, 174; Isabelle Francais: pages 2, 4, 5, 7, 8, 12, 13, 15, 18, 24, 28, 30, 31, 41, 44, 51, 53, 54, 56, 59, 63, 67, 68, 73, 75, 83, 85, 86, 89, 92, 114, 118, 121, 122, 125, 128, 136, 139, 140, 143, 145, 146, 148, 156, 170, 171, 177, 179, 180, 184; Daniel Johnson: page 158; Paulette Johnson: pages 17, 57, 108, 130 131, 132, 134, 135, 155, 159, 163, 167, 173, 188, 189; Connie Summers: pages 32, 34, 42, 169.

Cover Photos

Shutterstock: front cover, back cover, inside front cover, inside back cover.

All inquiries should be addressed to:
Barron's Educational Series, Inc.
250 Wireless Boulevard
Hauppauge, New York 11788
www.barronseduc.com

ISBN-13: 978-0-7641-4317-5
ISBN-10: 0-7641-4317-4

Library of Congress Catalog Card No. 2010923194

Printed in China

9 8 7 6 5 4 3 2 1

Important Note

When you handle cats, you may sometimes get scratched or bitten. If this happens, have a doctor treat the injuries immediately.

Make sure your cat receives all the necessary shots and dewormings; otherwise serious danger to the animal and to human health may arise. A few diseases and parasites can be communicated to humans. If your cat shows any signs of illness, you should definitely consult a veterinarian. If you are worried about your own health, see your doctor and tell him or her that you have cats.

Some people have allergic reactions to cats. If you think you might be allergic, see your doctor before you get a cat.

It is possible for a cat to cause damage to someone else's property and even to cause accidents. For your own protection you should make sure your insurance covers such eventualities, and you should definitely have liability insurance.

Contents

Preface   vi

1. **A Brief History of Cats and Cat Breeds**   1
   Where Cats Came From   1
   Coming to America   3
   How the Cat Fancy Began   4
   How Cat Breeds Get Recognized   6
   The Breeds   8
   Long- and Shorthaired Cats   8
   Mutations   12
   Colors and Patterns   13

2. **Acquiring a Cat**   16
   What to Consider First   16
   Lifestyle Considerations   22
   Where to Find the Right Cat   25
   Buying from a Pet Store   29
   Buying a Purebred Cat   30
   Choosing a Healthy Cat or Kitten   34

3. **Bringing Your Cat Home**   36
   Cat Supplies   36
   Cat-proofing Your Home   46
   Hazards in the Yard   48
   Holiday Hazards   50
   Introducing a Cat to Other Pets   52
   Cats and Kids   54
   Cat Care While You're Away   56
   Pet Identification   57
   When Things Don't Work Out   58

4. **Feeding Your Cat: Feline Nutrition Basics**   59
    The Carnivorous Cat   59
    Commercial Cat Foods   60
    The Nutrients Cats Need   63
    Minerals and Urinary Tract Health   72
    Preservatives and Other Additives   74
    Life-Cycle Nutrition   76
    Making Dietary Changes   81
    Deciphering a Cat Food Label   82
    Feeding Guidelines   85
    Are Homemade Diets Okay?   86
    Avoiding Finicky Behavior   87
    The Importance of Water   87
    What Not to Feed Your Cat   88

5. **Keeping Your Cat Fit**   94
    Fat Cats   94
    Signs of Obesity   95
    Weight-Loss Formula Cat Foods   100
    Putting a Fat Cat on a Safe Diet   101
    Exercising Your Cat   103

6. **Keeping Your Cat Healthy**   106
    Choosing a Veterinarian   106
    Signs of Illness in the Cat   106
    Preventive Health Care   108
    Feline Diseases   113
    Internal Parasites   119
    External Parasites   122
    Feline Vital Signs   127
    Allergies in Cats   127
    Feline Dental Care   128
    Medicating Your Cat   130
    Preventing Hair Balls   132
    Feline First Aid   133
    Euthanasia and Pet Loss   136

7. **Grooming Your Cat**   138
    The Purpose of Fur   138
    Benefits of Grooming   138
    Seasonal Shedding   139

Grooming Tools 140
Introduction to Grooming 140
Trimming Claws 143
Bathing Your Cat 144

8. Understanding Your Cat 147
Cat Language 147
The Cat's Primary Senses 150
Balance and the Righting Reflex 154
Sleeping Habits 155
Hunting Habits 155
Territorial Marking Behaviors 157
Handling House-soiling 160
Social Behaviors in Multicat Households 164

9. How Cats Reproduce 166
Spaying and Neutering 166
The Feline Facts of Life 166
Preparing for Birth 168
Delivering Kittens 169
Trouble Signs During Birth 171
Kitten Development 172
Basic Feline Genetics 175
Professional Breeding Strategies 176
Registering a Purebred Litter 177

10. Showing Your Cat 178
Breed Standards 178
How a Cat Show Is Organized 179
Types of Shows and Classes 180
Getting Started in Cat Shows 182
The Day of the Show 184
Traveling to Shows with Your Cat 185
Responsible Pet Ownership 187

Useful Addresses and Literature 188

Index 192

Preface

Cats enrich our lives in many ways. They provide companionship and unconditional love. They satisfy our need to nurture and care for something other than ourselves. Their playful antics make us laugh, and their contented purring can help us feel relaxed and at ease. In fact, experts say that taking care of a cat, or any pet, can be good for us.

So in return for all cats give us, we owe it to them to provide the best care possible. Within the pages of this book, you will find answers to many questions you may have about selecting and caring for a cat, such as

- where to find the right cat for you,
- how to keep your cat healthy,
- what to feed your cat,
- why cats behave the way they do,
- how to get involved in showing your cat.

This book is intended to be a general reference and guide to cat care and selection; however, it should never serve as a substitute for the advice of your veterinarian. While every effort has been made to help ensure that the information contained herein is accurate and up-to-date, please keep in mind that medical opinions and treatments can change over time as more advanced scientific knowledge becomes available. So when you have questions or concerns about your cat's health, nutrition, behavior, or overall well-being, always consult your veterinarian.

In addition, read as much as you can about cat care. There are many reference books and magazines available, and some of them are listed in the back of this book. Frequent reading on the subject of cat care also will help you stay up-to-date on the latest findings in the field.

Finally, responsible pet ownership requires knowledge and commitment. With proper care, your cat is likely to share your home and your life for at least a decade or more. A good way to prepare yourself for such a long-term commitment is to learn as much as you can about what you're getting into beforehand. To that end, this book aims to be a useful reference.

Chapter One

A Brief History of Cats and Cat Breeds

Where Cats Came From

Charming and intelligent, cats have been humankind's companions for centuries, long before feline enthusiasts began to selectively breed and develop purebred bloodlines. All domestic cats, from the fanciest purebred seen in show halls to the random-bred alley cat, have common origins, descending from just a few wild progenitors. Most experts agree that the modern cat, *Felis catus,* likely descends from a shorthaired wildcat, called *Felis lybica,* that roamed the plains of ancient Africa and western Asia. Many of today's tabbies still retain the distinctive striped markings, and the lithe, muscular body of this wild ancestor.

Domestication

Unlike most wild animals, *Felis lybica* often chose to live near human settlements and hunt the vermin that would inevitably seek out and raid the food stores. As a result, the cat gradually accepted domestication as a reasonable trade-off for the privilege of staying close to an easy and stable food source. However, the cat was one of the last of our modern-day animals to be domesticated, lagging far behind the dog, which became man's hunting companion some 16,000 years ago.

History generally credits the Egyptians with being among the first people to domesticate the cat approximately 3,500 to 5,000 years ago. Astute agriculturists, the Egyptians most certainly recognized the cat's inestimable value in protecting their grain stores from rats and mice. One might imagine that the Egyptians began enticing these prowling wild felines to stay close to their settlements, perhaps by leaving scraps of food near their grain stores. As a result, taming or *domestication* of wild cats gradually took place. So valuable was their natural pest-control service that cats enjoyed an extended period of elevated status during this early era of human civilization. In fact, archaeological discoveries suggest that Egyptians worshipped cats as representatives

of household gods. The Egyptian goddess, Bast, was often depicted as a woman with a cat's head. So revered were these animals that symbolized their religious beliefs that Egyptians mourned the loss when a cat died, and even mummified the animal's remains for entry into the afterlife. As one may guess, the penalty for killing a cat in those days was death.

Supporting the theory of Egyptian domestication and African origins is the fact that many of today's domestic shorthaired cats remarkably resemble the stately Egyptian cats depicted in ancient paintings and sculptures. Likewise, some of their longhaired cousins, with their tufted ears and cheeks, retain the lynxlike look of their wild African ancestor, *Felis lybica*.

From Gods to Devils

Not all cultures worshipped cats as gods, however, the way the Egyptians did. By the Middle Ages, cats had spread to European nations, transported there no doubt by traders who, realizing their worth, carried specimens back to their homelands for rodent control. The thirteenth century proved to be a bleak time for cats. Along with their human associates accused of witchcraft by the Christian Church, cats became symbols of evil, devil worship, and pagan practices. As a result, they were persecuted, tortured, burned, and killed in the cruelest ways.

The Black Death: In one of the subtle ironies of history, retribution for this unjust sentencing came swiftly in the form of the Black Death, which fell upon western Europe in the mid-1300s and, within approximately four years, wiped out nearly half of the human population there. The Black Death was the bubonic plague, a deadly bacterial infection spread by disease-bearing rodents and the fleas that live off their blood. The bite of an infected flea transmitted the disease from rat to man.

In retrospect, experts have suggested that the deliberate and systematic elimination of cats from the unsanitary streets and crowded towns of Europe during this time may have helped contribute to the rapid spread of bubonic plague. Unaware of the relationship between rats, fleas, and the plague, people caught up in the misguided religious and political fervor of the time effectively reduced the cat population that was helping to keep the rodents under control. In exercising this serious error in judgment, they may have unwittingly tipped the odds in favor of a devastating epidemic.

In time, the Black Death ran its course, but not without incurring profound social changes that would signal the end of the Middle Ages. The persecution of cats eventually ended as well, as people once again came to appreciate their role in reducing rodent populations. At the dawn of a modern age, the domestic cat emerged from one of the darkest chapters in world history to begin a new journey into the heart of humankind.

Cats today: Today, cats are the most popular pets in North America, outnumbering dogs per household by nearly two to one. And while most modern house cats no longer find it necessary to serve primarily as mousers, they continue to enrich our lives as companions and in countless other ways.

Coming to America

While we know that domestic cats were in Europe by the Middle Ages, no one knows for sure exactly when they first arrived in the New World. Cats may have crossed the ocean as early as the Vikings or Columbus, but by the 1600s they were most certainly coming along for the ride with European immigrants aboard sailing ships. The breed lore of the American Shorthair cat even mentions the *Mayflower* as one possible mode of transport. Such a tale is not implausible, since cats were brought along on long sea voyages in those days to hunt the rats and mice that ate the ship's food supplies. Owing to this practice, North America's domestic cats probably are descendants of cats brought from the British Isles and other western European countries.

Upon arrival in the New World, the cats were released to extend their pest-control duties in and around the new farms and colonies being settled. For centuries, these working mousers flourished in the fields and barns of America's pioneers, allowing natural selection to mold them and multiplying into a durable, diversified lot.

How the Cat Fancy Began

By the late 1800s people had begun to view cats as more than mere mousers. As cat shows and the *cat fancy*—the collective term used to describe those interested in breeding and showing purebred cats—developed first in England, then spread to America, cats gained popularity as companion animals. People even began importing exotic breeds, such as longhaired and Siamese cats, from abroad. Some of these cats were allowed to run free and mingle with the domestic shorthair stock already flourishing on native soil. As a result, kittens began to appear with varying coat lengths, color patterns, and temperaments, lending even more diversity to the melting pot.

A *purebred* cat, of course, is bred from members of a recognized breed or its allowable outcrosses and has a recorded ancestry. A non-pedigreed or *mixed-breed* cat, on the other hand, is generally understood to be the feline equivalent of what canine enthusiasts affectionately refer to as a mutt. While sometimes it may be obvious that one parent was of a specific breed, such as a Siamese, the mixed-breed cat's ancestry is, in most cases, unknown and unverifiable.

Today, the more politically correct and probably the more accurate term for cats of uncertain ancestry is *random bred.* Language purists may argue that the term mixed breed more properly means that at least two recognized breeds have been mixed or crossbred—say, a purebred Persian was mated with an American Shorthair, or a Russian Blue was crossed with an Abyssinian to produce offspring. Yet, the more common reference—mixed breed—remains well understood by the general populace to mean a little bit of this and a little dash of that, with who knows what else added for extra flair.

First cat show: With the rise of the cat fancy came the cat shows. Harrison Weir staged the first cat show in 1871 at London's Crystal Palace. Weir also developed the first breed standards by which cats were judged in those days and served as president of Great Britain's first national cat club, which issued the first feline stud book in the late 1800s.

The United States was quick to follow Great Britain's lead, as cat exhibits and judgings have taken place here since the 1870s. But an official all-breed show held in 1895 at New York's Madison Square Garden marked the real beginning of interest among North American cat fanciers. In 1899 the first and oldest U.S. cat registry, the American Cat Association (ACA), was formed to keep records.

Today, numerous cat-registering associations exist in North America. They include the Cat Fanciers' Association (CFA), the American Cat Fanciers' Association (ACFA), the International Cat Association (TICA), the Cat Fanciers' Federation (CFF), the American Association of Cat Enthusiasts (AACE), the National Cat Fanciers' Association (NCFA), the United Feline Organization (UFO), the Canadian Cat Association (CCA), and the Traditional Cat Association (TCA). Each association has its own show rules and breed standards, but all maintain stud books, register pure-bred cats, and verify pedigrees. Most of them also charter clubs, sanction shows, and present awards and titles. CFA, incorporated in 1919, is the world's largest registry of pedigreed cats, sponsoring approximately 400 shows a year across the United States and internationally through its more than 650 member clubs.

While preference is given to pure-bred cats in the cat show world, most associations sponsor house-

Show Your Cat

Whether you have a purebred or a random-bred household pet that you want to show, you typically must register the cat with the association sanctioning the event. The association uses the registration information to score and track awards. For more information on showing your cat, please see pages 178–187.

hold pet (HHP) categories in which random-bred cats and kittens can compete and earn awards (see page 182). HHP classes existed as early as the mid-1960s, but they were primarily sideshows to the purebred competition, judged by a local disc jockey or someone other than a qualified judge. Often, the so-called judge considered it more fun to choose the meanest, fattest, or strangest-looking cat, a practice that actually demeaned the mixed-breed cat. The Happy Household Pet Cat Club, founded in 1968, and a group of its exhibitors from the Sacramento, California, area were instrumental in changing this by lobbying for fairer standards and equality in judging for HHPs. As a result, TICA was the first association to license HHP specialty judges.

Today, the awards and show procedures for HHP competition are more in line with purebred competition. TICA, ACFA, CFF, AACE, UFO, and TCA also maintain registries for nonpedigreed household pets. The world's largest association, CFA,

does not register non-purebreds, but many CFA-sponsored shows and clubs do have household pet categories that also award year-end honors to the top winners. The Happy Household Pet Cat Club, an international organization open to all feline fanciers, also registers random-bred cats, which allows its members to submit cat show scores and claim titles.

How Cat Breeds Get Recognized

A breed is a group of cats that share predictable characteristics in conformation, coat type, color, and temperament. Representatives of a particular breed are judged against a written standard of perfection, called the *breed standard,* which describes the common characteristics that are considered ideal for the breed.

Some breeds originate in a particular geographic region. The Turkish Angora and the Turkish Van are native to Turkey, as their names imply, and the Siamese cat originated in Siam, now called Thailand. But other breeds, like the Somali, may be named for regions to which they have no real ties. The Somali, often described as a longhaired Abyssinian, was named after modern-day Somalia, also known as Ethiopia, but the breed does not hail from that part of the world. Rather, the name was chosen symbolically, because Somalia borders the ancient African kingdom of Abyssinia, for which the Somali's sister breed, the Abyssinian, was named. There again, the Abyssinian cat is named, not for its national origin (because no one is certain where the Aby really came from), but for the first such cat shown in England, a cat named Zula that was imported from Abyssinia around 1868.

New breeds, or new varieties and colors of existing ones, are being developed all the time. Some breeds, like the short-legged Munchkin, may begin as spontaneous genetic mutations, while others are created by crossbreeding established breeds. For example, the snub-nosed Exotic Shorthair, often called the "lazy man's Persian" because of its short, low-maintenance coat, is the hybrid result of crossing two recognized breeds, the American Shorthair and the Persian.

Whatever the origin, the process of achieving recognition among the cat fancy for each new breed is typically a long and arduous task that can take years. The rules for acceptance vary among the cat fancy associations, but generally, proponents of a new breed start by applying for registration. Once cats are accepted for registration, a certain number have to be registered over a period of time before they can begin showing in noncompetitive, miscellaneous, or nonchampionship classes for experimental breeds and colors. Called Any Other Variety (AOV) or New Breeds and Colors (NBC), such classes are designed specifically for new breeds with new standards and

for pedigreed cats that do not conform in some way, usually in color or coat length, to their current breed standard. In this prechampionship phase, new breeds hold provisional status and are judged according to a provisional standard. Proponents of the new breed must see that a certain number of cats continue to be registered and shown before full recognition is granted. Achieving the final step, championship status, requires the concerted effort of many breeders over a period of time before their cats become eligible to com-

pete for points and awards in championship classes.

The Breeds

The chart beginning on page 9 lists the breeds currently recognized in North America by one or more of the cat-registering associations. Most of the breeds hold championship status in various associations, which means they can compete at shows for awards and titles. Other breeds, being new or experimental, may be accepted for registration and shown in new breed and color classes, or they may hold provisional status until they can compete in championship classes.

Long- and Shorthaired Cats

The world has more shorthaired cats than longhairs for a sound, scientific reason. In the absence of purposeful or isolated breeding, natural selection in most regions seems to have tipped the odds in favor of the shorthaired cat over the longhaired variety. This is because the gene that produces a short coat is *dominant,* while the gene for a long coat is always *recessive.* Dominant genes are so named because they tend to suppress or mask the qualities of any recessive genes that may be present.

A kitten inherits one gene for coat length from each parent. This means that, to be born with short hair, a kitten has to inherit a dominant gene for this trait from at least one parent. To be born with long hair, a kitten must inherit two recessive genes for this trait—one from *each* parent. These basic genetic principles apply to any breed.

The kitten that inherits a shorthaired gene from one parent and a longhaired gene from the other will be a shorthaired cat, even though he carries a hidden or unexpressed longhair gene. Due to the dominance of the shorthaired gene, the gene for long hair is not expressed. However, a shorthaired cat that carries both types of genes is capable of producing either short- or longhaired offspring when paired with a mate carrying like genes. Cats that carry genes for both long and short hair are genetically *heterozygous.*

Cat Breeds

Abyssinian	A slender, shorthaired breed famous for its "ticked" or agouti coat
American Curl	Shorthaired and longhaired varieties that sport ears that curl backward
American Bobtail	A naturally occurring short-tailed cat that comes in all colors
American Shorthair	Formerly the Domestic Shorthair, with plush, short fur and a rounded face
American Wirehair	Similar to the American Shorthair, except for its coarse, crimped, springy, wiry coat
Balinese	The longhaired version of the Siamese cat
Bengal	A spotted, man-made hybrid resulting from an Asian leopard cat-domestic cat cross
Birman	Called the Sacred Cat of Burma, a longhaired, pointed breed that has four white paws
Bombay	A jet black, shorthaired breed with gold or copper-colored eyes
British Shorthair	Great Britain's native shorthaired cat that comes in many colors, most commonly blue
Burmese	"Copper Cat" from Burma that is noted for its glossy, rich, dark brown, short coat
California Spangled	A shorthaired spotted cat that resembles a miniature leopard
Chartreux	A blue-gray-colored, short-coated cat known as the "smiling cat of France"
Chausie	A large, long-bodied, cat resembling its wild ancestor, the Jungle cat of Thailand
Chantilly/Tiffany	A longhaired cat that comes in chocolate brown and several other colors
Colorpoint Shorthair	Like the Siamese in most aspects, a cat that comes in more colors
Cornish Rex	A breed that has short, soft, wavy hair as its distinguishing feature
Cymric	The longhaired version of the Manx cat

Cat Breeds (continued)

Devon Rex	Discovered in Devon, England, a cat that has a thin, wavy coat and curly whiskers
Donskoy	A Russian hairless breed that is often born coated but generally loses its hair within the first year
Egyptian Mau	A spotted tabby (the word *mau* means "cat" in ancient Egyptian)
European Burmese	Similar to the American Burmese, but available in more colors
Exotic Shorthair	A shorthaired version of the Persian cat, recognized as a separate breed
Havana Brown	Shorthaired cats from Siam with rich, burnished brown coats and green eyes
Himalayan	A Persian cat with Siamese-type colorpoint markings
Japanese Bobtail	Short- and longhaired varieties noted for their bunnylike bobbed tails
Javanese	Another Siamese-type cat that is the longhaired version of the Colorpoint Shorthair
Kurilian Bobtail	A natural short-tailed breed, occurring in short- and longhaired varieties, that is native to the Sakhalin and Kuril Islands of Russia
Korat	A silvery-blue short-coated cat originating in Thailand
La Perm	A curly-coated American breed with short or long hair that falls in loose ringlets
Maine Coon	An American breed prized for its heavy, shaggy coat and large size
Manx	A shorthaired, tailless cat that originated on the Isle of Man in the Irish Sea
Minskin	A short-legged, sparsely haired breed with fur "points" on the face, ears, nose, legs, and tail
Munchkin	A short-legged cat whose long body and low-slung posture resembles that of a ferret
Nebelung	A blue cat with a silky, medium-long coat and silver-tipped guard hairs

Cat Breeds (continued)

Norwegian Forest Cat	A longhaired cat from Norway that is among the largest of domestic breeds
Ocicat	An American breed of shorthaired cat with leopardlike spots and an agouti coat
Ojos Azules	"Blue eyes" in Spanish, this cat's most notable physical feature
Oriental	Built like the Siamese, a breed that comes in more colors and in both coat lengths
Persian	A longhaired cat with rounded head and eyes and flat face and nose
Pixie-Bob	A new domestic short-tailed cat that is visually similar to the bobcat
Ragdoll	A longhaired cat typically marked with dark points and white mittens and blaze
RagaMuffin	A cat that shares the Ragdoll's background but is recognized and shown in many more colors
Russian Blue	A blue cat with green eyes and plush, double-coated short fur
Savannah	A spotted cat that resulted from a cross between the wild African Serval and a domestic shorthair
Scottish Fold	A breed with shorthaired and longhaired varieties that sport forward-folded ears
Selkirk Rex	A curly-coated cat that comes in both long- and shorthaired varieties
Serengeti	A wild-looking, usually spotted cat developed by crossing the Bengal with Oriental shorthairs
Siamese	A colorpoint shorthaired breed from Siam (Thailand), with a long, slender body
Siberian	A large, longhaired cat from northern Russia similar to the Norwegian Forest Cat
Singapura	The smallest of domestic breeds, an agouti-patterned cat from Singapore
Snowshoe	An American shorthaired breed with colorpoint markings and white feet

Sokoke	A shorthaired cat sporting a distinctive, ticked tabby coat, native to Kenya, Africa
Somali	The longhaired version of the ticked-coated or agouti-patterned Abyssinian cat
Sphynx	A slender, big-eared, hairless breed produced by a spontaneous genetic mutation
Thai	Also referred to as the "old-style Siamese," this breed is dedicated to preserving the natural pointed cat that is native to Thailand today.
Tonkinese	Once called the Golden Siamese, a shorthaired cat that is a Siamese/Burmese cross
Toyger	The result of a Bengal and domestic shorthair cross, this cat with bold, randomly placed vertical stripes truly resembles a miniature or "toy" tiger.
Turkish Angora	Although most commonly white, longhaired cats that come in many other colors
Turkish Van	Longhaired white cats with color occurring in the Van pattern on the head and tail
York Chocolate	A chocolate-colored cat with a medium-long coat

Cats that have only longhair genes or only shorthair genes are said to be *homozygous* for that trait. The beautiful longhaired Persian cats, for example, are homozygous because they must possess two longhair genes before the recessive longhair trait can express itself. Consequently, Persians, when bred to other longhairs, always produce longhaired offspring.

Mutations

Occasionally, genes go haywire as nature attempts to improve upon itself or create something new and better suited to the environment. Aside from color variations, genetic mutations are also responsible for other distinctive characteristics certain breeds bear, such as the folded ears of the Scottish Fold, the stubby tail of the Manx, the hairless coat of the Sphynx, and the soft, curly coat of the Devon Rex and the Cornish Rex. Selective breeding has preserved these mutant traits that under random conditions likely would have disappeared with the influence of dominant genes or other factors.

Colors and Patterns

For show purposes, colors are grouped by division and include solids, silvers, shadeds and smokes, colorpoints, tabbies, particolors, and bi-colors. Solids are sometimes referred to as *self* colors. Tabbies have a pattern of stripes, patches, and bars. Silvers, shadeds, smokes have darker-tipped hairs lying against a paler ground color or undercoat color, which gives the coat a contrasting, shimmering effect, especially when the cat moves and the fur parts. *Particolor* is a broad term for a coat of two or more colors, such as a tortoiseshell, which is black with patches of red. A *bi-color* has a coat of two colors, one of which is white.

While many purebreds are bred specifically for their coloring, all of the beautiful colors, patterns, and markings that can be maintained by selective breeding can also appear randomly in the mixed genetic bag that makes up our treasured stock of nonpedigreed, domestic cats. And even though our modern-day domestic cats come in varying coat lengths, colors, and color patterns, they all are genetically tabbies, like their wild African ancestors. The term "tabby" commonly refers to the familiar striped color pattern, not to a specific breed. The pattern occurs in purebred and random-bred cats.

Bars and stripes: Most people recognize the tabby as a cat that has pronounced stripes and bars on its coat, tail, and legs, and frown marks that form an intricate "M" on the forehead.

• The classic or blotched tabby has wide stripes, swirls, patches or blotches, often forming a recognizable bull's-eye pattern on the sides.

• The more common mackerel tabby has thinner stripes running from the backbone down the sides resembling fish ribs, hence the name.

• The rare spotted tabby, as the name implies, sports spots instead of stripes. The stripes are actually there, but they are broken in places so that they resemble spots.

The agouti pattern: There also are tabbies with no stripes at all. The Abyssinian and Somali breeds represent a unique form of tabby without stripes called the agouti pattern. These two closely related breeds— one a shorthaired type, the other a longhair—are noted for their reddish brown hair ticked with bands of darker color. The ticking, or agouti pattern, results from alternating light- and dark-colored bands on each hair shaft, giving the coat a delicately flecked appearance. The pattern occurs in some other species as well, as in squirrels, and serves as excellent camouflage.

Tabby colors: Of the tabby varieties, the most common colors are

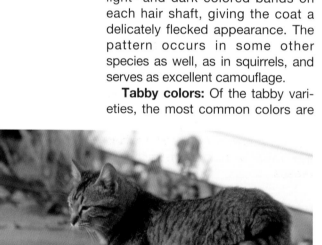

the red tabby (sometimes called orange, yellow, or ginger), which bears deep, rich red markings against a lighter red or yellow ground color; the silver or gray tabby, which sports black stripes against a silver or gray background; and the brown tabby, which has black markings on a reddish brown background.

But if all cats are genetically tabbies, how did we end up with the plethora of colors and patterns we see in domestic cats today? Well, over time, genetic changes have occurred that, depending on how genes are arranged in a particular individual, may result in masking or suppressing the distinctive tabby markings; yet, some variation of the tabby gene remains present in all cats. If a cat inherits genes that completely mask the stripes and bars, he will be a self or solid color, such as solid black, for example. But underneath, the cat is still a tabby.

Dilute colors: Generally speaking, dominant genes tend to produce darker, denser colors, such as black or red (also called orange), while recessive genes, in the right combination, will produce dilute colors that are paler than their dominant counterparts. For example, the color gray, which cat fanciers call blue, is the recessive or dilute form of black. Likewise, a cream-colored cat is a paler shade of dominant red.

Spots and patches: There are many patterns that produce interesting color combinations in cats. A common genetic occurrence referred

to as the white spotting factor randomly applies splashes of white to the face, feet, and belly, or, in the case of the calico cat, draws dramatic white patches among intermingling blotches of black and orange. Interestingly, calicos and tortoiseshells, which have a patchwork of black and orange blotches like the calico, but without the white, are nearly always females. The lovely patchwork of black and orange is a sex-linked trait produced by genes carried on the female (XX) chromosomes (page 176).

Colorpoints: The pointed pattern, characterized by darker points on the cat's face, tail, feet, and ears against a lighter body color, predictably appears in certain purebred cats, such as the Siamese, the Himalayan, the Birman, the Ragdoll, the Balinese, and the Snowshoe. This recessive trait is also known as the Himalayan pattern, named after the Himalayan rabbits that sport the same coloration. It is frequently called the Siamese pattern, too, and while perhaps best known because of Siamese purebreds, the pattern occasionally crops up in random-bred cats as well. Cat fanciers often refer to cats with these markings as *colorpoints.* The gene that produces the pointed pattern is linked with another trait that produces the blue eye color common in the colorpoint breeds.

Interestingly, pointed kittens are born looking nearly white. Their points gradually darken with age. Cooler temperatures influence the pigmentation and darkening process as well, which, experts say, explains why kittens remain light-colored until they exit their mother's warm womb. After birth, the extremities normally stay a degree or two cooler than the body's core, so these furthermost points tend to darken more.

Chapter Two

Acquiring a Cat

What to Consider First

Acquiring a cat or kitten should never be an impulse decision. Important things to consider before you adopt or purchase one include the financial and legal responsibilities of pet ownership, your living and working arrangements, and any friends and family members who may be allergic to cats. You also should try to match the temperament of the cat to your own lifestyle and personality preferences, whenever possible. For example, if you're considering buying a purebred, would a highly energetic and vocal animal, like a Siamese, drive you crazy? Or would you prefer a quieter, more sedate, passive personality, such as the Persian, as your household companion? Here are some other questions to consider before you get a cat:

Indoor or Outdoor Cat?

First, decide whether you prefer to own a cat that stays indoors all the time or one that goes outside. If you want an outside cat, it makes sense to adopt one that is already accustomed to living outdoors. Some people insist on letting their cats roam freely because they believe that depriving cats of their outdoor freedom is cruel. But most experts agree that cats kept indoors live longer, healthier lives.

Cats that live their lives totally indoors are less likely to be exposed to diseases, plagued by parasites, hit by cars, attacked by dogs, killed by coyotes, bitten by wild animals, caught in wild animal traps, poisoned by pesticides, and harmed by cruel people.

You can also expect to have fewer veterinary bills related to injuries from cat fights and similar mishaps, if you keep your cat indoors. In addition, you will have peace of mind, knowing that your well-cared-for indoor cat has a smaller chance of contracting illness or parasites, such as Lyme disease-carrying ticks, that could affect you or your family.

Keeping your cat indoors will also help ensure that he has the best opportunity to live out his full life expectancy. As long as you provide love and attention, your cat will be quite happy and well adjusted living indoors. If you feel your cat must experience the outdoors, supervise outings in the yard, build an outdoor exercise run, or install a cat flap that provides safe access to a screened-in porch.

Purebred or Mixed-breed Cat?

Many people who consider acquiring a cat as a companion wrestle with the question of whether they should adopt a homeless cat from a shelter or invest in a pedigreed animal whose temperament and appearance are more predictable. To some, this is a real ethical dilemma, given that there are so many unwanted cats destroyed each year simply because there aren't enough homes to go around for all of them. For every purebred purchased, they reason, a homeless cat loses its chance to be adopted.

Regardless of whether you choose a purebred or a random-bred cat, you are still offering a good home to an animal that can become your valued companion. And aside from the expense of acquisition, the costs of caring for a random-bred versus a purebred cat are virtually the same as far as cat food, veterinary care, and routine vaccinations are concerned.

Ultimately, your choice depends on what you're really looking for in a cat. Certainly, random-bred cats make just as good companions as purebred felines. Also, the so-called alley cat is much less expensive to acquire. But where mixed-breed cats are purely potluck, purebreds,

on the other hand, have a recorded ancestry, called a *pedigree.* The advantage in knowing a cat's family history means that certain health factors and other important qualities can be predicted with greater accuracy. In acquiring a kitten with papers, you'll have a general idea about what he's going to grow up to look like and about what kind of personality he will possess as an adult.

If your ultimate goal is to show cats, you'll most certainly want a purebred to register and compete in championship classes. Keep in mind, however, that most major cat shows also have a special household pet category for exhibiting non-pedigreed, random-bred cats. In

household pet classes, cats are judged according to their beauty, condition, and personality rather than a written breed standard. Typically, the associations that sponsor household pet divisions require that cats entered in this category be spayed or neutered.

Many cats exhibited in the household pet category have heartwarming stories behind them about being rescued or adopted from shelters. And, no doubt, many seasoned cat show exhibitors got their start showing in this category, learning the rules of the trade along the way.

One Cat or Two?

If your lifestyle and financial situation permit, acquiring two cats can be the perfect solution to the dilemma of whether to invest in a purebred or to adopt a nonpedi-

greed cat. Why not get one of each, as long as you can afford the double cost of caring for two animals?

Like people, cats can become bored and lonely when forced to stay alone all day while you are away at work. One way to avoid this problem is to get two kittens at the same time, and at about the same age, so they can bond as friends and keep each other company. Besides, two cats are twice as much fun to watch. Once acquainted, the two will romp and play and give each other exercise.

Adult Cat or a Kitten?

Kittens are cute and adorable, and few people want to miss the joys of this short-lived stage. However, you can save yourself the expense of spaying or neutering by adopting a grown or nearly grown cat that already has been altered.

If your heart is set on a purebred, you may get lucky and find one that is being retired early from a breeding program or the show ring. Such cats typically cost less to acquire than a purebred kitten, simply because it is harder to sell adults or find good homes for them. Usually, purebred cats placed in this way are altered and up to date on their annual vaccinations prior to sale, saving you, the buyer, these initial expenses.

Certainly, kittenhood holds special joys for cat lovers, but this stage can also be the most destructive. Kittens are not born knowing how you expect them to behave in your home. They have to be properly socialized and patiently taught not to climb your draperies and not to sharpen their claws on your couch.

On the other hand, many adult cats are surrendered for adoption because of behavior problems related to their past care or to a lack of proper socialization and training. House-soiling and destructive clawing are two of the most common behavior problems that result in cats being surrendered to animal shelters for adoption (see page 25 for tips on adopting a cat from a shelter).

Male or Female?

Unless you intend to become a professional cat breeder, the sex of the cat you choose as your companion should not matter. If you simply want a household pet, both males and females make equally fine companions after you alter them—that is, once you spay a female or neuter a male cat. If your interest is focused on the show ring, remember that even purebreds can be shown at cat shows in alter classes, also called premiership classes, after they have been spayed or neutered.

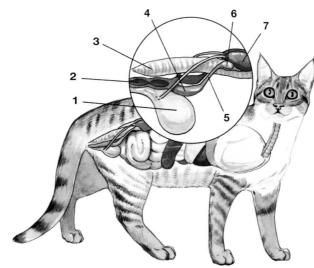

1. Bladder
2. Vagina
3. Rectum
4. Uterus
5. Fallopian tube
6. Ovary
7. Kidneys

The internal reproductive organs of the female cat.

When to spay or neuter: Veterinarians traditionally recommend that male cats be neutered between eight and ten months of age and that females be spayed at six months, but both surgical procedures can now be performed safely at a much earlier age. In fact, to ensure that indiscriminate breeding does not take place, some shelters and breeders may elect to spay or neuter kittens early, *before* they go to new homes. Studies have suggested that the practice of early spaying and neutering appears to be safe and does not adversely affect feline maturity, as was once thought.

Generally, early spaying can take place between 12 and 14 weeks, and early neutering can be performed between 10 and 12 weeks. If you are interested in altering your kitten early, discuss the issue with your veterinarian.

Why bother to alter at all? Choosing a male cat is the strategy some people use to avoid being saddled with raising unwanted litters of kittens and having to find homes for them. Yet, they don't give a second thought to letting their intact male roam freely to breed indiscriminately with other cats. Such irresponsible pet ownership only contributes to the existing pet overpopulation crisis and the annual surplus of unwanted, homeless pets that must be euthanized.

About 75 percent of cats taken into U.S. animal shelters are humanely put to death each year, simply because there aren't enough homes to go around for so many. Annual humane death figures have

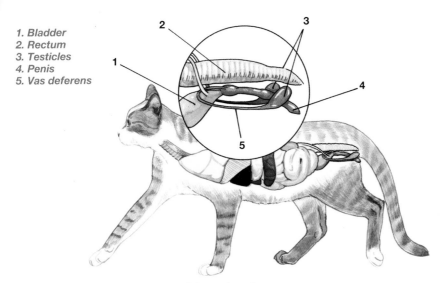

1. Bladder
2. Rectum
3. Testicles
4. Penis
5. Vas deferens

The internal reproductive organs of the male cat.

fluctuated from a staggering 4.3 million to nearly 9.5 million within just the last decade. Countless other homeless cats fall victim to neglect, starvation, and other hazards of life in the wild. To help control this tragic waste of life, responsible cat owners make it their moral duty to prevent indiscriminate breeding either by not allowing intact cats to roam freely or by having their male *and* female cats altered.

Is altering beneficial in other ways? Yes, aside from the social and moral responsibility, there are other good reasons to spay and neuter. In the male cat, neutering reduces aggressive behaviors, eliminates testicular diseases, and decreases the chance of certain other diseases occurring later in glands affected by male hormones. Neutering also helps

curb the male cat's bothersome tendency to spray urine in the house to mark his territory.

In the female cat, spaying eliminates the female's annoying heat periods along with her ability to have kittens. The operation also eliminates the possibility of any disease or infections in the organs removed and decreases the chance that breast cancer will occur later in life.

In addition to these health benefits, altering a male or female cat reduces the animal's natural desire to leave the relative safety of its territory and search for a suitable mate. Eliminating this biological urge makes the animal a much nicer companion and, along with keeping the cat indoors, improves its chances of living a longer, healthier life. Animals allowed outside to roam freely in

Cost Concerns

Many communities have low-cost spaying and neutering programs available through local humane organizations. So, if spaying or neutering costs are a big concern for you, ask your veterinarian or your area animal shelter to refer you to such a program.

search of mates are more likely to be killed by cars, injured in fights, or exposed to contagious diseases, and you'll likely be faced with repeated veterinary bills for treating the injuries your cat incurs. These bills can quickly exceed the one-time cost of spaying or neutering, so it makes good financial sense to alter your cat and keep it safely inside.

Will altering make cats fat? Contrary to popular myth, spaying or neutering will not make your cat grow fat and lazy. As in people, overweight problems in cats are caused primarily by too much food and too little exercise. *Obesity* (see page 95) is a medical condition involving an overaccumulation of body fat. A fat cat is, in many cases, the result of an overabundance of treats, and consistent overfeeding by its owner.

What about the costs of altering? Spaying a female cat costs more than neutering a male, because the female operation involves opening the abdomen to remove the ovaries, tubes, and uterus. In contrast, neutering the male cat is a less invasive procedure that involves

removing the testicles. Both surgical procedures require anesthesia, but the postoperative, in-hospital recovery period is generally shorter for males than for females. Certainly, the one-time cost of spaying a female is considerably less than the long-term cost and responsibility of raising and finding homes for successive litters of kittens.

Lifestyle Considerations

Having considered the pros and cons of a purebred versus a mixed-breed cat, an adult versus a kitten, male versus female, and so forth, it should now be obvious why acquiring a cat demands some careful planning and forethought. After all, you are adding a new member to your family that will require your care for years to come—perhaps a decade or two. You want to make sure you find a cat that will be a good fit for the way you live, as well as where you live. Following are some other equally important points to consider:

Your future plans: Acquiring a cat deserves a commitment on your part to take care of the animal's needs from kittenhood through old age. With modern veterinary care and good nutrition, more cats are living longer, an average 10 to 15 years, so look ahead into your own future and ask yourself if you will be willing and able to provide your cat with shelter, food, and regular veterinary care. Of course, predicting the future is impossible, but you can make some reasonable guesses. For example, if you anticipate that a future job change or promotion might require you to move across or out of the country, perhaps you should postpone getting that adorable cat or kitten, unless, of course, you're absolutely certain you can take the animal with you when you move. Likewise, if marriage is in your future, make sure your intended spouse likes cats and that your new lifestyle and living arrangement together can accommodate your pet.

Housing concerns: Make sure that your housing situation is suitable for owning a cat. In some situations, certain restrictions may apply to, or even prohibit, the keeping of pets. Sneaking a pet into a rented residence without permission or without first checking out the rules could get you both evicted. If you rent, your landlord may require an additional fee, plus a pet damage deposit in case your cat claws the draperies or carpets. This practice is neither uncommon nor unreasonable. As a cat owner, you are liable and responsible for any property damage or personal injuries your animal may cause. To avoid hassles, find out what rules and ordinances apply in your area, then decide whether you can comply fully, before you acquire a cat.

Travel and time spent away: Animals, like children, need special attention and someone to look after them when you're not around, so before acquiring a cat, consider how much time you normally spend away

from home. If you travel often, do you have a trusted friend or relative who is willing to care for your cat while you're away? If not, can you afford to board your cat or hire a pet-sitter to care for him while you're away? Are you home enough to spend quality time with your cat and give him the love and attention he needs and deserves? If not, owning a cat, or any pet, could become a constant source of worry and guilt for you, especially if you tend to feel bad about not being able to spend enough time with your pet.

Pet allergies: Many people are allergic to cats, some more than others. Unfortunately, many cats are surrendered to animal shelters each year because their allergic owners cannot tolerate the severity of their allergy symptoms. Proteins produced by the cat's salivary and sebaceous (fatty oil) glands trigger the allergic response. These proteins are deposited onto the cat's fur when the cat licks himself during grooming. When dry, the proteins flake into easily inhaled airborne particles called dander. This cat dander, rather than the cat itself, is the true allergen, or allergy-causing substance. The tiny particles settle primarily into carpets, draperies, upholstered furniture, mattresses, walls, and ceilings.

So, as you consider getting a cat, think about you and your family members' allergic tendencies. Even if you have no allergies, consider others close to you who may no longer feel comfortable visiting your home because their asthma or allergies worsen in the presence of felines. It would be grossly unfair to the cat if you had to give him away later simply because your social life suffers.

For the person who experiences only mild or intermittent allergy symptoms, certain compromises may allow a comfortable coexistence with cats. Suggested coping strategies include vacuuming frequently, replacing carpets with hard floors, replacing upholstered furniture with vinyl or leather, washing the cat in distilled water once a month, applying antiallergy wipes or sprays to the cat's fur, using an air purifier in the home, and keeping ductwork, furnace, and air-conditioning filters clean. Many people effectively manage their symptoms with various allergy medications or desensitizing allergy shots prescribed by their doctors.

Your age and health: Certainly, most people expect to outlive their pets, but this is not guaranteed. Consider what would happen to your cat if you died suddenly or became incapacitated by an injury or illness. Too often, an animal faces neglect, abuse, or abandonment if the owner has not planned ahead for its care in case of an emergency. This is especially true for pet owners who live alone. Give a trusted person advance instructions—and keys—to enter your property immediately and assume care of your cat if you should die suddenly or become disabled.

Your will and your cat: To further ensure that your pet will be cared for if something unexpected happens to you, include your cat in your will. More and more people are recognizing the importance of doing so. In fact, legal experts recommend that you will your cat outright to a friend or relative who has agreed in advance to comply with your wishes regarding its care. In your will, appoint that person as your cat's guardian. You also may wish to bequeath a modest sum of money to that person to cover the cost of your cat's care during its remaining years. For more information about wills and the laws in your state, consult a lawyer.

Where to Find the Right Cat

Once you've decided that you want a cat, and what type of cat you want, the next step is finding a suitable candidate. If papers and pedigrees are not important to you, you should not have to search far for a feline companion, as there is no shortage of random-bred cats in need of good homes. To begin, check your local animal shelters, humane society chapters, animal rescue organizations, or cat clubs. Larger organizations are usually listed in the telephone book or advertise in local newspapers. Most veterinarians' offices have information about such organizations, and many even post a list on their bulletin boards of pets needing homes. Other avenues to pursue include the classified section of your local newspaper, pet stores, or friends and neighbors with unplanned litters.

Adopting from a Shelter

An animal shelter is an excellent place to begin your search for a cat in need of a good home. While you're more likely to find random-bred cats there, even purebreds sometimes end up being surrendered to shelters for adoption.

Not all shelters are alike, however. Some are private or volunteer organizations, while others are funded by tax dollars and operated by city or county governments. Generally speaking, an animal control facility is a public institution that must accept any animal brought in. Some animal control facilities, especially those in poorer areas, operate on low budgets and have limited space, and as a result, may be forced to euthanize more animals than they are able to keep and place in homes. Private shelters and volunteer rescue organizations, on the other hand, are more likely to have a no-kill policy. Such organizations are able to exercise this policy by refusing to accept more animals once they reach capacity, or by using a network of foster homes where cats are cared for until they can be permanently placed.

Adoption practices vary widely, but most shelters will require that you fill out a questionnaire and sign a form agreeing to have the cat spayed or neutered, unless this already has been done. Often, by asking a few questions, the shelter workers can help you select a cat that has a temperament best suited to your own personality and lifestyle. Some shelters may even want to visit your home, to ensure that the cat will be housed and cared for properly. Do not be offended by organizations that attempt to investigate your suitability as a pet owner;

they are acting in the best interests of the animals they have sworn to protect.

Most shelters also request a donation or charge an adoption fee—usually no more than $50 or $60—to pay for the food and veterinary care the cat received there. If the organization had the animal spayed or neutered, the fee helps cover that cost as well. Another reason shelters charge a fee is that people naturally tend to place greater value on and take better care of a pet that they pay for, as opposed to one that is free.

High-end shelters, or those with bigger budgets to spend, sometimes screen their animals in advance for various parasites and diseases, and administer at least an initial series of vaccinations. Some even spay or neuter animals prior to adoption. Other organizations offer vouchers that can be redeemed at most veterinarians' offices for a free or discounted medical exam and spaying or neutering. Some shelters also operate information hot lines that you can call if you have general questions about cat care and behavior.

Before adopting from a shelter, find out as much as you can about the history and care that has been provided to the cat. For example:
• Under what circumstances did the animal arrive at the shelter?
• Has a veterinarian examined the cat?
• Has the cat received any vaccinations?
• Has he been checked or treated for internal parasites?

• Has he been tested and found to be negative for feline leukemia virus (FeLV) and feline immunodeficiency virus (FIV)?

Knowing these details is especially important if you have other cats at home. Usually, this information is spelled out in the contract or adoption agreement that you sign, but if not, always ask. In addition, make sure you understand the shelter's return policy, in case the animal you adopt turns out to be sick or simply doesn't work out in your home.

Taking in a Stray

Sometimes, it is the cat that finds and adopts a new owner, instead of the other way around. We've all heard variations of the typical scenario: A scraggly stray shows up on your doorstep, hungry, perhaps even hurt or sickly. The pathetic plight of such a homeless creature pulls at your heartstrings, so you set food out for him, which is, of course, an invitation to the cat to stay.

Countless cats are cruelly abandoned each year when their owners move, die, or simply grow tired of them and give them the boot. While it's hard to imagine how people can be so irresponsible and cold-hearted as to leave a cat on the side of the road or to move away and abandon the animal to fend for himself, the sad reality is that this happens all too often. Most homeless strays suffer a meager existence and eventually die from disease or starvation, or they end up being hit by cars or killed by other animals. Only a lucky few happen upon the yards and homes of kind-hearted folks who eventually take them in.

Before taking in a stray, however, make sure he is genuinely homeless, and not just a neighborhood pet looking for an extra handout. Ask around or advertise in the Lost and Found section of your newspaper. If the cat is lost, the original owner may come forward and claim him. If the cat is tame enough to let you safely handle him without him scratching and biting, check for any form of pet identification—collar, ear tag, or tattoo (usually on a rear inner thigh). Some owners have tiny microchips implanted between the pet's shoulder blades. These can be

detected by a special scanner, which your area's animal shelter may have.

If you do happen to find a homeless stray, there are some special precautions you should take.

• **Warning:** Assume that the cat has had no vaccinations, including rabies, and approach the animal cautiously, for your safety.

• Wear thick gloves if you handle or pick up the animal the first time. Many abandoned cats revert to the wild after only a short period without human contact, and they will fight fiercely if captured.

• If you have other cats, do not expose them to the stray until he has been checked by a veterinarian and quarantined from your animals for at least a week, preferably two, to make sure the stray isn't incubating a contagious disease. Before bringing the stray into your home,

capture him if you can do so safely and take him to a veterinarian immediately for a thorough examination.

• If you intend to keep the animal, request that he be checked for parasites and tested for FeLV and FIV. If the latter tests come back positive, you will be faced with a difficult decision, as you will not want to take an infected animal home and expose your other healthy cats to him. If you have no other cats at home, you will want to weigh the costs of providing ongoing medical care for a sick animal before you definitely decide to keep it. FeLV- and FIV-infected cats can live a long time with their chronic conditions. Your veterinarian can tell you what to expect.

• If the animal checks out as healthy, have him vaccinated for rabies and feline respiratory diseases right away, and follow any other vaccination plan your veterinarian recommends.

• If the cat is an intact male, have him neutered to reduce the incidence of spraying and fighting.

• In the case of a female foundling, it may be difficult to tell whether she has already been spayed. So, you may want to keep her inside and wait awhile to see whether she goes into heat or displays any signs of pregnancy.

Rescuing and Rehabilitating a Sickly Stray

If the cat you find is ill or malnourished, your veterinarian can recommend an appropriate treatment plan. If the stray appears to have a potentially contagious respiratory illness, you may want to consider boarding him at the clinic until he recovers, rather than risk exposing your other cats at home. This will also allow time for all of the necessary test results to come back.

If you've found an abandoned kitten, chances are he may be dehydrated and will require fluid replacement. If the kitten was orphaned at a young age and is weak from malnutrition and neglect, you may be in for a siege of round-the-clock feedings every few hours, as instructed by your veterinarian. Newborns must be fed every two or three hours, and because they cannot yet eliminate on their own, you will need to stimulate the anal area with a warm, moist washcloth after feeding. Normally, the mother cat performs this duty by licking her youngsters' bottoms with her rough, wet tongue. By about four weeks of age, kittens can control their own elimination. At that time, they also can begin experimenting with soft, solid foods (see page 76). Whatever the circumstances, your veterinarian can recommend an appropriate formula and feeding schedule.

The outcome of such rescues is always unpredictable, and sometimes downright sad, but the rewards can be potentially great, as the survivors often seem to comprehend their predicament. Eternally grateful to their human benefactors, these rescued cats often turn out to be the most devoted and loving companions of all.

Buying from a Pet Store

Although pet stores usually deal in purebred animals, some do take in unwanted mixed-breed kittens from local residents and sell them as a goodwill gesture. Others will house random-bred cats and kittens for local humane societies to improve their chances of adoption.

If you consider buying a cat from a pet store, ask how and where the shop acquired him. Try to find out as much as you can about the cat's history. If you're not satisfied with the answers you get, look elsewhere.

The staff should be able to tell you the age and sex of the kitten and give you correct advice on cat care. If you are satisfied that the staff seems knowledgeable, that the environment is clean, and that the cat or kitten appears healthy, then the pet store may be as good a place as any to acquire your new compan-

What to Look for at the Pet Store

Select a pet store that houses its animals in large cages comfortably furnished with beds, litter pans, toys, and food and water dishes. The accommodations should be clean and odor-free and closed off in such a way—preferably behind glass windows—that customers can look but cannot constantly disturb and handle the kittens.

ion. Just make sure the written purchase agreement includes a medical and vaccination history, as well as a guarantee that you can return the kitten if he develops health problems within a specified period of time.

Buying a Purebred Cat

If your heart is set on acquiring a purebred cat, there are several advantages to buying from a private, small-volume breeder. If the breeder is local or near the town or city you live in, you can visit the cattery and see firsthand the environment in which the kitten was born and raised. You also can see what the dam (the mother), and sometimes the sire (the father), of your kitten looks like. Usually, other cats from the same bloodline are present to give you a good idea of what your kitten's appearance and temperament will be like when grown. Also, when you buy from a small-volume breeder, you gain the opportunity to establish a relationship with someone who can share his or her experiences in raising and showing that particular breed.

Before you buy, first research the breed that interests you in order to learn about its temperament, genetics, and care. Some breeds, such as the Siamese and Abyssinian, are highly active and energetic, while others, such as the Persian, are noted for their quiet, passive personalities. Make sure the qualities inherent in a particular breed match your own personal preferences for a feline companion. For breed-specific information, read books or call one of the cat-registering associations and ask for a breed profile.

Then, to begin your search for a reputable breeder, call the various cat registries and ask for a list of people in or near your area who breed the type of cat you are looking for (see Useful Addresses and Literature on page 188). Peruse the ads and breeder directories published in the cat magazines. Attending cat shows is an especially good way to meet cat breeders, because you can talk to them in person and see firsthand the quality of their cats. Some breeders advertise in the classified sections of newspapers or pin their business cards on bulletin boards in veterinarians' offices.

If the cattery is within driving distance, visit and observe for yourself whether the facility is clean and free of pungent animal odors. Also note whether the cats are kept in cages or allowed to run about freely in an area of the house. While it is not unusual for breeders to keep their studs caged or to confine kittens for their own safety when unattended, it is highly preferable to acquire a kitten that has been allowed to explore its surroundings and socialize with people and other cats. In fact, experts say that kittens gently handled by people at an early age tend to grow up to be better people-oriented pets.

Questions a Breeder May Ask You

Responsible breeders always try to make sure their kittens are going to good homes, where they will be wanted, loved, and treated well. A conscientious breeder will ask potential buyers certain questions that reveal a lot about a person's attitude and knowledge about pet ownership. Expect such questions as:

• Do you intend to keep your cat indoors? (Some breeders will not sell their kittens to people who want outdoor cats.)

• Have you owned cats before? Was your previous cat spayed or neutered? (Some breeders may stipulate in their sales agreements that kittens sold as pets must be altered and not used for breeding.)

• Did you provide annual medical care for your previous cat? What happened to your previous cat?

• Do you own other pets now?

Such questions are not intended to make you feel intimidated, insulted, or defensive, so do not feel offended if a breeder interrogates you in this manner. Instead, recognize that you have been fortunate to locate someone who sincerely cares about the welfare of his or her cats. Breeders of this caliber feel that each kitten they raise represents a significant financial and emotional investment. They want to help other people become responsible pet owners and expand their general

knowledge of cats. They also want you to consider your cat as a valuable investment, a cat that will become your priceless companion and a member of the family.

Questions You Should Ask the Breeder

Here are some questions you should ask before the sales transaction becomes final:

• What cat association(s) do you use to register your cats? Ask to see the pedigree.

• What vaccinations has the kitten or cat received?

• Ask for the dates when the shots were given.

• Has the kitten or cat been tested and found to be free of feline leukemia virus (FeLV) and feline immunodeficiency virus (FIV)? Ask for copies of the animal's health records.

Purebred Pricing

The cost of a purebred cat can vary widely depending on the breed you're trying to acquire, availability (some breeds have waiting lists), geographic location, bloodlines, gender, and color, among other factors. Breeders typically structure their pricing according to whether an individual cat is pet quality, breeder quality, show quality, or *top* show quality. Cats in each category are purebred and fully registrable in the cat associations.

Pet-quality purebreds are the most affordable. If you have no real interest in showing or breeding cats and you simply want a nice pure-bred companion, then a pet-quality animal is your smartest buy. The pet-quality designation in no way means that the cat or kitten is less healthy or less desirable to own than a show-quality animal. It simply means that, in the breeder's opinion, some minor cosmetic flaw makes the cat unsuitable for show ring competition.

Breeder-quality cats also fail to meet the show standard in some small way, yet they possess enough good qualities, in addition to their excellent pedigree, to produce potentially outstanding offspring. Breeder-quality kittens are typically priced in the middle range, selling for somewhat less than their show-quality littermates, but for more than a pet-quality animal. Of course, the only reason to spend the extra money to buy a breeder-quality cat is if you plan to breed. In fact, some breeders will sell their breeder-quality cats only to other experienced breeders.

Show-quality cats are the most expensive to buy. Breeders consider their show-quality kittens to be outstanding examples of the breed, based on the breed's written standard, and they anticipate that such kittens will perform well in the show ring. Few breeders will sell a *top* show cat—or one that shows considerable show ring promise—to a novice owner.

If you're interested in buying a kitten for show, carefully study its pedi-gree. If the kitten comes from a line of champions or grand champions, those cats' names will be prefixed by Ch. or Gr. Ch. The more grand champion titles that appear in the first two or three generations of a kitten's ancestry, the better the chances that the kitten, too, may grow up to be a winner.

The Sales Agreement

A written sales contract describes all terms of the sale, including the purchase price and payment schedule, the breeder's health guarantee, and any neuter/spay requirement. Contracts vary from breeder to breeder; however, all agreements should spell out the buyer's option to return the kitten and get his or her money back if the kitten is found to be unhealthy or unsuitable within a specified period after purchase.

Health records and vaccination certificates should accompany the sales agreement. To save money, some breeders vaccinate their own kittens, which is a legal practice. However, in areas where rabies shots are required for cats, the vaccine must usually be administered in the presence of a state authority, such as a veterinarian or an animal control officer, before a legal certificate can be issued. When shipping kittens by air, health and rabies certificates are typically required, depending on the destination and on the airline's regulations.

Papers and Registration

The purchase price should include the kitten's papers and pedigree.

Because pedigrees can be verified by the cat-registering associations, a purebred's papers provide proof of his parentage. Remember, you are paying for the predictable qualities that a certain bloodline offers. On the other hand, it's important to understand that papers alone do not guarantee the health or quality of a kitten.

Depending upon the arrangements of the sale, the seller may rightfully withhold the papers or registration slip until the buyer furnishes proof that the cat has been spayed or neutered. While registration matters most to breeders, because it ensures that an animal's progeny will be registrable as well, registering a cat also enables you to show him in purebred competition classes, if you choose to do so.

Choosing a Healthy Cat or Kitten

Whether you buy from a pet store, adopt from a shelter, answer a classified newspaper advertisement, purchase a purebred, or select a kitten from a neighbor's litter, the animal you choose should have good muscle tone and bright, clear eyes, and he should be alert and friendly with a curious or playful attitude. A healthy cat or kitten should not be sneezing or showing mucus discharge around the eyes or nose. The ears should be clean and free of dark, crusty wax. Head shaking or ear scratching may indicate ear mites or other infections. The anus should be clean and free of any signs of diarrhea.

The environment where the cat or kitten has been kept should be clean and free of pungent animal odors. The animal's coat also should be clean and free of fleas. To inspect the coat for fleas, rub your hand against the fur and look for fine grains of black dirt, which is really dried flea excrement, called "flea dirt" (see page 122). Flea signs are more prevalent behind the ears, on the back and at the tail base, where the cat cannot easily reach to lick clean.

To test the cat's personality, tempt him with a feather or ribbon and see how playful and relaxed he is around strangers. If he appears fearful, hisses at you, cringes from your hand, or, in general, seems unused to being handled, you may want to look elsewhere for a better socialized animal. Of course, a shy, withdrawn cat that huddles quietly at the back of the cage at the animal shelter may come out of his shell and adapt successfully to life with a single adult or a quiet couple. If you have a house full of children, however, you will want to look for an outgoing, unflappable cat, one that sits at the front of the cage and reaches out his paw for attention.

Medical History

Once you've selected a cat or kitten, ask if he has been tested for FeLV and FIV, as noted previously. If the cat has not been tested, you will want to make sure he is free of these diseases before introducing him to other cats you may have at home. If any medical or vaccination records are available, ask for copies. Have your veterinarian examine the animal within a day or two after you take him home to help ensure that you've picked a healthy one.

Age: Knowing a kitten's age is important, too. Kittens taken away too young from their original surroundings sometimes suffer from stress and have trouble adjusting to a new environment. Some also may develop unusual behavioral problems related to their maladjustment.

Ideally, a kitten should not leave his original environment until he is between 8 and 16 weeks old. Many breeders of purebreds will not release their kittens to new homes until they are between 12 and 16 weeks old. By this time, a kitten has been weaned and litter-trained, is eating solid food, and, depending on the owner, may have had some or all of his first year's vaccination series. This is a best-case scenario that may be possible if, for example, you are planning to adopt a kitten from a friend or neighbor's unplanned litter. However, since space at animal shelters is scarce, kittens there typically go to new homes by about eight weeks of age, or as soon as they are weaned and eating solid food.

In cases in which a breeder must ship a kitten to you, the animal must be at least three to four months old to conform with most airline age requirements. The breeder usually helps with shipping arrangements, but you can expect to pay all costs.

Chapter Three

Bringing Your Cat Home

Cat Supplies

Bringing home a new cat or kitten is an exciting time for the whole family, but the sudden change to new surroundings may be somewhat intimidating from the new arrival's viewpoint. To make your cat's transition to his new home as comfortable as possible, a little planning and preparation are in order. Plan to make the event as quiet as possible. Avoid bringing home a new cat or kitten during a holiday because such times are usually too hectic and busy, and the added noise and visitors will only upset and frighten the newcomer. Give the animal a few days to adjust to his new surroundings before inviting visitors over to see him.

Following is a list of basic pet supplies you'll need to have on hand when your kitten arrives:
• Food and water dishes
• Cat or kitten food
• Pet carrier
• Litter box
• Cat litter
• Litter scoop
• Cat bed
• Scratching post
• Cat toys
• Grooming supplies

Food and Water Dishes

Every pet in the household should have his own feeding dish, so select one ahead of time for your new cat and decide on a feeding location. If you have other pets, and you're concerned about them eating the newcomer's food, feed the cat or kitten in a separate area, at least until he gets better adjusted to his new surroundings. Or, if you have a dog that tends to steal cat food, you may need to place an adult cat's dish on a countertop or table, where the cat can jump up and eat, out of the dog's reach.

What type of dishes should you select? Stainless steel, ceramic stoneware, or glass dishes, although more expensive than plastic feeding bowls, are generally easier to keep clean because they can be sterilized in the dishwasher without melting or warping. Ceramic dishes come in decorative varieties, but select only the ones sold for human use or labeled as lead-free. Otherwise, you have no way of knowing whether the paints and glazes used on the dish contain harmful lead that may leach into your cat's food or water.

Plastic dishes are cheaper and come in a variety of colors and shapes. While many people use the plastics with no problems whatsoever, cat owners should be aware of the following two main drawbacks associated with plastic dishes:

1. Some cats may become allergy-sensitive to the chemicals used to make plastic dishes. While this is a relatively rare occurrence, cats that are allergy-sensitive will display itchy bald spots and crusty sores around the mouth and nose. If your cat develops such symptoms, discontinue use of plastic feeding dishes and consult a veterinarian for appropriate treatment.

2. Plastic dishes also tend to develop tiny pits and scratches over time, that can harbor bacteria and odors, despite diligent cleaning. The stale food odors that collect in these minute crevices may go unnoticed by the human nose, but your cat, with his more highly developed sense of smell, may find the odor buildup offensive enough to refuse to eat. To deter odor buildup, buy plastic dishes that are dishwasher-safe so they can be heat sterilized between meals. Another sound precaution is to replace plastic dishes with new ones periodically.

When selecting feeding dishes, keep in mind that most cats seem to prefer flat, shallow saucers or plates to deep bowls. Apparently, cats dislike having their sensitive whiskers rub the sides of the dish as they eat. In fact, some cats dislike this unpleasant sensation so much that they will resort to scooping out food morsels with their paws and eating off the floor.

Also, choose a weighted food dish that's heavy enough to stay put and not slide across the floor as the cat eats. Imagine how frustrating your meals would be if your plate kept sliding across the table every time you tried to take a bite!

Always wash feeding bowls after meals, and replenish water daily. In hot weather, cats love a few ice cubes added to their water as a cool treat.

Self-feeders, which handily dispense food from a bulk hopper as the cat dines, and self-waterers are convenient gadgets to have for those times when you must be away overnight. Some owners use them routinely for leaving out dry food for their cats to nibble on free-choice or *ad libitum* throughout the day. If you choose to feed this way, here are a few concerns to consider:

1. Dry food left out too long in this manner can become stale and lose some of its nutritional value. To avoid this, replenish the amount daily—or at least every other day—with fresh food stored in a sealed pouch or container.

2. Dry food left out too long also may attract insects, so inspect the bowl and contents for this problem each time you refill.

3. While routine bulk feeding may be convenient, the practice can encourage overeating and contribute to obesity. Of course, free-choice feeding of dry food is okay, as long as you are careful not to overfeed (see page 97). If your cat tends to overeat, however, it is better to measure out one day's allowance of dry food and leave it in a bowl for the cat to eat at will, rather than supplying a steady overabundance of food via a bulk feeder.

Self-waterers dispense water from an inverted bottle into a dish as the cat drinks. Be warned, however, that cats, being intelligent and playful creatures, can quickly discover

how much fun it is to shovel out water or kibble with their paws simply to watch the liquid bubble or the food fall! While your cat may never engage in this particular sport, it is important to be aware that, during one playful spree, a cat can potentially empty a full self-feeder or self-waterer all over your kitchen floor in a matter of minutes, leaving you to clean up the mess.

Pet Carriers

To bring your cat or kitten home, you'll need a suitable pet carrier for the animal to travel in safely. A carrier is a sound investment because you'll use it to cart your cat to the veterinarian's office, grooming and boarding facilities, or cat shows. Available through catalogs, pet supply stores, and sometimes veterinarians' offices, pet carriers range from inexpensive fold-out cardboard boxes to the sturdier molded plastic ones. There are also decorative wicker baskets, canvas totebag varieties, and heavy-duty airline-approved types that can be used when cats must be shipped by air. Regardless of the carrier type you select, it should fasten securely and be well ventilated, so that the animal inside cannot escape but can get plenty of fresh, circulating air.

If you have more than one cat, each animal should have its own carrier for safe transport. Avoid putting two cats together in a single carrier, even if they are best friends. The too-tight quarters and the stress of travel might cause them to fight and injure one another.

Litter Boxes

A litter box is essential equipment for any cat that spends time indoors. Pet stores and mail-order catalogs carry a wide variety of litter boxes, from the basic open plastic models to the fancy ones with ventilated bottoms and pull-out trays. The more expensive ventilated designs allow air to circulate beneath a tray to help dry the urine. These designs are a plus for helping to control cat box odors. Covered litter boxes also help contain odors and give shy cats privacy, but some cats seem to dislike the confinement. For a young kitten's shorter legs, start with a shallow litter box with low sides, then switch to a larger size pan as the cat grows.

Cleanliness: Regardless of the kind of litter box you select, it's important to keep the box clean, or the cat may stop using it if it becomes too soiled (see page 163). You'll also need a litter scoop to remove solid wastes from the box daily. At least once a week, clean the box with hot water and refill with fresh litter. Keeping the box fastidiously clean and changing the litter frequently are the best ways of controlling litter box odor in your home and making sure that the cat continues to use the box. A little bit of baking soda mixed into the litter also helps control odor in close quarters, or try one of several commercial cat box odor control products available at pet supply and grocery stores.

Location of the box: For privacy, place the litter box in a quiet, undisturbed area of the house. Do not place it too near the cat's food dishes or sleeping quarters. Being fastidious creatures, cats normally do not like to eat or sleep near the place where they relieve themselves.

More than one box: If you have more than one cat, provide each with its own litter box, and place the pans in separate locations, if necessary. Although cat friends will often share litter boxes, some more aggressive cats may chase others away in a show of dominance. Without an alternate box to use, the subordinate cat may have no choice but to use the carpet or some other inappropriate place.

Litter box training: By the time your new kitten is old enough to leave his mother and go to his new home, he should already know how to use a litter box. The instinctive digging and covering behaviors come naturally to cats, and they learn the rest by observing and imitating their mothers. Orphaned kittens, however, lack this training from their mothers and, as a result, may be slower to learn to use the litter box, or they may develop sloppy litter box habits.

But for kittens that have spent their first several weeks of life with their mother and siblings, potty training, or house-training in a new environment is usually a breeze. Generally, all you have to do is show the kitten where his new litter box is. Do this when you first bring the kitten home. Set him in the litter box and gently move his front paws in the litter in a scratching motion. Repeat this, as needed, after the kitten's first few meals in his new surroundings, and he should quickly catch onto the idea.

If the kitten seems slow to catch on, confine him temporarily to a small area with a litter box, until he does his business. Sometimes adding a single drop of ammonia to the litter helps. The scent of ammonia, being a by-product of urine, usually attracts cats to use the spot as a potty.

Cat litters: Litter selection is important, because if your cat doesn't like the texture or scent of the type you choose, he may refuse to use the box. Some cats dislike the perfumed or chemically treated pellets added to commercial litters for odor control. These additives may please human noses, but cats seem to prefer their own urine scent. For really finicky felines, plain, untreated clay litter or sterilized sand may be better choices. Avoid using dirt from the yard or garden, however, as it may contain insect larvae or other unwanted organisms, including the one that causes toxoplasmosis (see page 55).

Trackless litters: These are designed to stick less to a cat's paws, thereby reducing the number of granules tracked outside the box onto your carpets and floors. For greater economy, certain litter brands can be rinsed and reused, but most cannot be flushed down the toilet. So, to avoid wrecking your bathroom plumbing, read product labels carefully, if the product doesn't say it's flushable, it probably isn't.

Clumping litters: Some litter brands are designed to clump when moistened. These are popular and convenient, because it is easy to scoop out clumps of urine along with the solid wastes. This clumping action aids greatly in sanitation and odor control by leaving behind only clean, fresh litter.

Certain clumping brands have an unfortunate tendency to stick to a cat's fur, although many manufacturers have worked to correct this problem. So, if you have a long-haired cat, inspect the backside and hind legs on occasion to make sure litter is not sticking to its fur.

In addition, concerns have been raised about clumping litters causing digestive blockages, if swallowed. As a precaution, avoid using a clumping litter with young kittens, as they are more likely than adults to sample the stuff by tasting and eating it. When your cat is grown, switch to a convenient clumping brand if you like.

Cat Beds

Most cats like to select their own sleeping places and will alternate their napping spots on a whim. More than likely, your cat's preferred siesta site will probably be your bed or your favorite chair. Many people like to share their beds with their cats; however, if you want to discourage your cat from sleeping with you, keep your bedroom door closed or confine your cat to a certain area of the house during the night.

Regardless of your sleeping arrangements, you should provide your cat with his own bed. Whether you buy a plush, fancy *cat cozy* from the pet store or simply throw an old blanket in a cardboard box, select something washable, because you want to be able to launder your cat's bedding frequently. Also, since many cats prefer high places, you may be more likely to persuade your cat to use his bed if you place it on an easily accessible shelf or table, rather than on the floor.

Scratching Posts

A sturdy scratching post is another essential piece of equip-

ment for cats confined to the indoors. Cats have an instinctive need to scratch and sharpen their claws on objects in their territory. Even declawed cats continue to display this natural feline behavior. The action not only removes dead nail and reconditions the claws, but also marks territory with scent from glands in the paw pads. The scent left behind on the object draws the cat back to the same spot to scratch time after time. Obviously, this can pose a problem if your cat starts clawing your furniture. You cannot eliminate the cat's natural instinct to sharpen claws, but you can modify the behavior by providing your cat with an alternative scratching post. Pet stores and pet supply catalogs sell scratching posts in many shapes and sizes, or, if you're handy with tools, you may wish to build your own.

Carpeted cat trees: These extend from floor to ceiling, make attractive scratching posts, and come in all colors to match any room's decor. A tree that combines sisal rope and carpet satisfies the scratching preferences of most cats. Creative designs incorporate built-in perches and peekaboo penthouses for catnapping. Not only do they double as lofty sleeping quarters, they offer ample exercise and climbing opportunities for indoor cats. And because most cats like to be near their human companions, they are more likely to use a scratching post or climbing tree located in the room where the humans spend most of their time.

Selecting a scratching post: Before introducing your cat to his scratching post, make sure the post isn't wobbly and won't tip over as the cat claws it. Stability is the most important feature to consider when purchasing or building a scratching post. Obviously, if a flimsy, unstable post falls over and frightens your cat, the animal likely will refuse to go near it ever again, and understandably so. The base must be wide and supportive enough to remain standing and balanced, even when accosted by the full weight of a clawing, jumping, or climbing adult cat. The scratching post also needs to be tall enough to allow a full-grown cat to stretch upward on his hind legs to his full length. A well-built kitty-condo-style scratching post can cost as much as $100 or more, but the investment is worthwhile in terms of sparing your

Scratching post surfaces: Some cats show a strong preference for bare wood stumps or tough tree bark. Others readily accept carpet-covered or sisal-covered man-made scratching posts as a substitute for tree trunks. Some prefer a flat, horizontal surface, such as a thickly carpeted floor, while others prefer a vertical, upright surface, such as a couch arm. Pay attention to how your cat scratches and to what he likes to use when he sharpens his claws. If your cat indicates a strong preference either way, and you supply the opposite, the cat may reject the type of post you provide. Be prepared to experiment with different varieties before you find one your cat will use.

home furnishings from the ravages of claws.

Cat Toys

Indoor cats need toys to play with, but you don't have to spend a lot of money on them. Cats can amuse themselves with ordinary items you might use in your own recreational pursuits, such as Ping-Pong balls, golf balls, and tennis balls. Leftover wrapping paper (but *not* the ribbons!) and paper grocery bags are a great favorite, too, but *never* use plastic bags for this purpose or leave them unattended around your cat, because cats, like children, may suffocate in them.

Supervise all access to fishing pole-style toys with feathers, sparklers, and tied-on lures. These interactive toys provide great exercise in your watchful presence, but if left unattended, the attached line poses a potential hazard for being chewed or swallowed, for accidental strangulation, or for wrapping too tightly around a limb and cutting off circulation. Always shut these types of toys safely away in a closet or cabinet when you're not around to play with your cat.

String and yarn: String of any kind is a definite no-no for cats, so do not offer yarn balls or threaded spools as toys. If you use such items in crafts or hobbies, store them safely out of reach of your cat. Also, be careful of braided rugs or knitted afghans that might unravel if the cat plays with a loose end. Once a cat starts chewing and swallowing string

Selecting Safe Toys

When selecting toys at the pet store, consider safety first. Choose only sturdy toys that won't disintegrate after the first few mock attacks. Remove tied-on bells, plastic eyes, button noses, and dangling strings that your cat could tear off and swallow or choke on during play. Never let your cat play with small items that could be chewed or easily swallowed, such as buttons, bows, hairpins, rubber bands, wire bread-wrapper ties, paper clips, cellophane, or wadded-up candy wrappers.

or yarn, a considerable amount may amass in the digestive tract and cause life-threatening blockages or perforations. If you come home to find your cat with a piece of string hanging out of his mouth, *do not* attempt to pull it out. Doing so can

cause more serious, even fatal, injury, if the string has already wound its way into the intestinal tract. Seek veterinary help immediately. Such a situation constitutes a true emergency. Surgery may be required to correct the ensuing condition, called string enteritis.

Catnip: A member of the mint family, catnip is a perennial herb that many cats go wild over. When exposed to a catnip-scented toy, a cat will grip the object in his front paws, rub his face in the fabric, and roll ecstatically, kicking at the object with the back paws. Afterward, the cat lies sprawled on his back, as if drunk, and dozes off in a relaxed, trancelike state of bliss, purring loudly and contentedly.

The substance in the plant that elicits this response is called *nepeta-lactone*. The effect wears off in a short time and does not appear to compromise the cat's normal faculties. In fact, an unfamiliar sound will bring a catnip-intoxicated cat to his fully alert senses immediately. Pet stores offer an array of catnip mice, catnip sacks, and other catnip scented toys for your cat's pleasure. Some stores even sell planter kits so you can grow your own stand of catnip at home.

The catnip herb is not thought to be addictive or harmful to domestic cats, so it is a relatively safe way to entice even the most sedate feline into a feisty, albeit brief, bout of play. However, not all cats care for catnip, and many have only a mild response when exposed to it. Some cats lack the gene that makes them respond to the plant's intoxicating effects, and they show no marked reaction when confronted with catnip.

Grooming Supplies

Whether you have a shorthaired cat or a longhaired one, regular combing and brushing will benefit you both by helping to control shedding in your home and by keeping your cat's coat looking clean, healthy, and mat-free. While long-haired cats shed about the same amount as shorthaired cats, long hair is more noticeable on your furnishings, carpets, and clothes; therefore, you can reasonably expect to become intimately acquainted with your vacuum cleaner, unless you make daily grooming a habit. Regular combing helps remove the loose hairs from your cat's coat before they have a chance to fall off onto your furniture. To easily wipe cat hair off your furnishings, keep a brush, lint remover, or a damp cloth handy.

To meet your cat's basic grooming needs:

• Invest in nail clippers (for humans or pets), several sizes of steel pet combs, and a natural bristle brush.

• For kittens, start grooming with small and medium-size steel combs, and save a wide-toothed one for use on adult cats.

• For flea control, purchase a fine-toothed comb. Once caught in the comb's closely spaced teeth, fleas drown easily when dipped in a pan of water. A fine comb also readily removes flea dirt deep in the fur.

• Talcum or baby powder helps remove oil and dirt from a cat's coat when sprinkled in and brushed out completely, but use powders sparingly and only when necessary.

Bath Supplies

For bathing your cat, select only pet shampoos labeled as *safe for use on cats.* Avoid dishwashing detergents, laundry soaps, or human shampoos. Never use dog shampoos or dog flea products on cats, because the ingredients may be too harsh and concentrated for felines. In fact, it's wise not to expose your cat unnecessarily to the insecticide ingredients in flea shampoos for cats, unless your cat needs to be treated for fleas. For details on bathing and grooming your cat, please refer to the section starting on page 138.

Window Perches

These carpeted shelves that attach easily to windowsills are an added luxury item that can give your indoor cat an eye to the outside world and provide a handy place to doze in the sun. To heighten your cat's pleasure, as well as your own, place a bird feeder or birdbath in view of the window, and your cat will be mesmerized for hours, as if watching cat TV. You'll have just as much fun watching your cat watch the birds!

To prevent falls and escapes, make sure all window screens lock in place and are sturdy, tight, and secure enough to withstand a grown cat's weight if he lunges at a fluttering insect on the outside. This is especially important if your house has a second story, or if you live in a high-rise apartment building. Although cats are well known for their ability to right themselves in midair and land on their feet, veterinarians treat enough injured cats that fall or jump from upper-story windows to give the condition a descriptive name—high-rise syndrome.

Cat-proofing Your Home

Once you've acquired the basic pet supplies for your new feline companion, you'll need to cat-proof your home, to make sure the environment will be safe. We've all heard horror stories about cats that drink spilled antifreeze from puddles in the driveway, then get sick and die. But cats don't have to drink poisons to get sick, nor are outdoor cats the only ones subject to potential harm. Many indoor hazards exist, too.

Because cats are such clean creatures, they can ingest wax, bleach, detergents, and other toxic

chemicals stored inside your home simply by brushing against a dirty storage container, or walking through a spill, then licking the offending substance off their paws and fur as they self-groom. With this in mind, take an inventory of all household chemicals and other potential hazards in your home that a climbing, exploring cat might have access to.

While it's hard to think of everything, be creative when you are scanning your home for potential hazards. To make your home cat-safe, do the same things you would do to make it child-safe. Whatever might harm a young child could also harm a cat. Get down on your hands and knees and look at each room from a cat's or a child's perspective, thinking about things that could pose a danger, such as dangling appliance cords or open sump pumps.

Here are some suggestions for cat-proofing your home:

Electric cords: The risk of electric shock is one of the greatest hazards found inside the home. Chewing on electrical cords can result in burns and electric shock. A cat playing with a dangling cord can topple a lamp or pull an appliance off a counter onto himself. To prevent this, tuck electrical and telephone cords out of reach under mats or carpets, tack or tape them down, or cover them with PVC piping. Coating cords with bitter apple, bitter lime (available at pet stores), raw onion juice, or Tabasco sauce also helps discourage chewing. If electric shock does occur, disconnect the current before touching the cat, or use a wooden broom handle to disengage the cat from the wire. Even if the cat appears to suffer only minor burns to the tongue and mouth, consult a veterinarian immediately. Complications from electric shock may not be apparent right away.

Drapery cords: Keep window and drapery cords tied up and well out of reach, as a frolicking feline can become entangled in dangling cords and accidentally hang or strangle himself.

Flimsy screening: Make sure all window and door screens are strong, sturdy, and secure enough to prevent a cat from pushing them out or falling through them.

Fireplaces: Securely screen fireplaces so that, when in use, cats seeking warmth cannot get too near the flames.

Household chemicals: Store cleaners, laundry detergents, fabric softeners, solvents, mothballs, insect sprays, and all other household chemicals out of reach in securely closed cabinets.

Cosmetics and medicines: Keep perfumes, cosmetics, nail polish removers, and all vitamins and medicines, including aspirin and acetaminophen (highly toxic to cats), tightly capped and put away.

String and hobby supplies: Put away pins, needles, yarns, spools of thread, artists' paints, and other hobby and crafts supplies when not in use to prevent a curious cat from investigating them and accidentally swallowing something harmful.

Hazardous toys: Certain children's toys can pose potential dangers to your cat. For example, an indoor basketball hoop placed over a trash can may trap a curious kitten that climbs or falls into the netting, causing accidental strangulation.

Vermin bait: Avoid using edible rodent and insect baits where your cat might get at them and get poisoned.

Breakables: Remove or secure all glass or breakable items on tables, shelves, and bookcases that an exploring cat might knock over.

Toilets and sump pumps: Keep toilet lids down and cover sump pumps so that kittens can't fall in and drown.

Appliances: Before shutting the door of any major appliance, such as the dryer or refrigerator, look to make sure a nosy cat hasn't jumped in unnoticed. Unplug small appliances when not in use. The dangling cords from a coffeepot or hot iron left unattended present a tempting hazard to a playful cat.

Stoves and countertops: Supervise all kitchen activities. With a cat in the house, no countertop is safe from exploring paws. If an inquisitive cat should leap up on the stove top when you're not looking, he can get burned accidentally by stepping on a hot burner or by sniffing a boiling saucepan or teakettle.

Trash cans: Keep tight-fitting lids on all indoor and outdoor trash bins so that foraging cats won't get sick from spoiled foodstuffs or injured by discarded razor blades, broken glass, or jagged tin can edges.

Hazards in the Yard

Even though you may have wisely decided to keep your cat safely indoors, there may be times when you will want to allow him outside for short periods while under your supervision, such as going for a walk around the yard on a leash (see page 105). When you do so, be aware that there are many potential hazards as close as your backyard and driveway. For example, many pesticides, weed killers, fungicides, and fertilizers can poison pets that walk in treated areas, then lick the chemicals off their paws. So read lawn care and pesticide product labels carefully before using, and avoid letting your cat outdoors to pad through freshly treated areas until the first rain or the next thorough watering has rinsed the substance away.

• Supervise pets around swimming pools and ponds, just as you would a child. Although cats can swim, kittens, especially, can drown from exhaustion if they fall in and can't find a way to climb out of the water.

• The driveway is another area where special precautions should be observed. Ethylene glycol, the prime ingredient in traditional antifreeze, is deadly poisonous to animals. As little as half a teaspoon can kill an adult cat. So if your car has even a tiny cooling system leak, you may put your own cat, or your neighbors' pets, at risk. To avoid this, immediately hose down or wipe up all fluid leaks and antifreeze spills, no matter how small. When adding fluids to your car, use a funnel to prevent spills.

Consider replacing your car's traditional antifreeze with a safer antifreeze brand. Safer antifreeze products on the market contain propylene glycol, which is significantly less toxic than ethylene glycol.

Hazardous Houseplants

Although carnivorous by nature, cats enjoy snacking on greenery, apparently because the added roughage aids in digestion. Unfortunately, cats often indulge this occasional craving by nibbling on decorative houseplants and ornamental shrubs. While many plants are harmless to cats, others are deadly. Ingestion can cause a wide range of symptoms, including mouth irritation, drooling, vomiting, diarrhea, hallucinations, convulsions, lethargy, and coma. If your cat displays any unusual behavior after chewing on a plant, consult a veterinarian immediately.

To make your house and yard cat-safe, avoid the following common toxic plants:

Besides nibbling on the greenery, it's also quite natural for a cat to mistake the dirt-filled base of a large potted house plant for a convenient litterbox. Unless you like your plants fertilized in this manner, cover the dirt with wire mesh or decorative rock.

Amaryllis	Daffodil	Jack-in-the-	Periwinkle
Asparagus Fern	Daphne	pulpit	Peyote
Azalea	Datura	Jerusalem Cherry	Philodendron
Belladonna	Delphinium	Jimsonweed	Poinsettia
Bird of paradise	Dieffenbachia	Larkspur	Pokeweed
Black locust	(Spotted Dumb	Lily of the Valley	Potato
Caladium	Cane)	Lupin	Rhododendron
Castor Bean	Elephant Ear	Marijuana	Rhubarb
Chinaberry	Foxglove	Mistletoe	Skunk Cabbage
Christmas	Hemlock	Monkshood	Spider Mum
Cherry	Henbane	Moonseed	Umbrella Plant
Christmas Rose	Holly	Morning Glory	Wild Cherry
Chrysanthemum	Honeysuckle	Mushrooms	Wisteria
Clematis	Hydrangea	Nightshade	Yew
Creeping Charlie	Iris	Nutmeg	
Crown of Thorns	Ivy	Oleander	

*The list is only a partial one; if you are unsure about a particular plant's toxicity, ask your veterinarian. The National Animal Poison Control Information Center also offers a comprehensive list of plants toxic to cats (see Useful Addresses and Literature on page 188).

In fact, propylene glycol is used as a preservative in some foods, alcoholic beverages, cosmetics, and pharmaceuticals. Even though your cat may be an indoor cat, using a safer antifreeze is a humane practice that can benefit free-roaming domestic animals and wildlife.

• Be aware that cats allowed outdoors in winter often crawl up under car hoods to sleep, because the engines stay warm hours after use. To alert sleeping cats, cautious people bang on the hood or blow the horn before starting the car. The fan blades and other engine parts can cause fatal injuries if an unsuspecting feline gets caught underneath. This is another good reason to keep your cat safely indoors and never allow him to roam freely, without supervision, outside.

Holiday Hazards

• Although accidental poisonings can happen any time of the year, they seem to be more prevalent during the year-end holidays. That's because cats like to investigate and sometimes sample the greenery commonly used for holiday decorations—poinsettia, holly berries, and mistletoe. These items can be irritating or toxic to cats, so either avoid using them, or restrict your cat's access to the decorated rooms.

• People often pose the greatest hazard to pets at holiday time. If your party guests tend to overindulge in the Yuletide spirits, stow your cat in a quiet, safe part of the house while you entertain. That way, no one will accidentally step on or stumble over your cat or, in a moment of poor judgment, be tempted to offer him a taste of something potentially toxic, such as alcohol.

• To prevent a curious, climbing cat from toppling a Christmas tree, anchor the tree to a wall or ceiling by tying it to a hook. And because baubles and bells on Christmas trees present an irresistible temptation to playful paws, use only unbreakable ornaments. Cats also love to eat the tinsel that dangles so alluringly from decorated trees. While not toxic, the stringlike foil can cause serious intestinal obstructions or perforations when swallowed, so avoid using it. Likewise, avoid angel hair, artificial snow, edible ornaments, and small plastic beads or berries that could be easily swallowed. Christmas wrapping ribbon can also pose the same threat as string if swallowed, or it can accidentally tie off circulation to a limb if the cat gets the ribbon too tightly wrapped around a leg during play.

• Aspirin and some commercial chemicals used as preservatives in Christmas tree water can be lethal to cats that might drink from the tree base. Avoid these chemicals, or keep cats out of the decorated room. Keep electrical cords on holiday decorations covered or out of reach, and unplug the Christmas tree lights when not in use. Leaving lighted candles unattended is unwise and unsafe at any time, as a frolicking cat might accidentally knock them over and start a fire.

• Chocolate also is toxic to cats, so never leave desserts and candy dishes exposed where your cat might sample the goodies when you're not looking.

• Resist the temptation to offer your cat holiday table scraps, because rich, highly seasoned foods can cause diarrhea and stomach upset.

• A few bits of cooked, unseasoned turkey at Thanksgiving is okay, but remove all bones, as these can get caught in the throat and cause your cat to choke. Jagged pieces of bone, if swallowed, can also perforate the gut, leading to life-threatening complications.

• Other holidays can be hazardous, too. Halloween, for example, is a dangerous time for cats allowed outdoors, especially black ones, because some fall victim to vicious pranks. Similarly, the noise of fireworks displays during the Fourth of July can frighten cats and cause them to run away.

Holiday or not, some people dislike cats so much that they may resort to deadly means to keep free-roaming ones out of their flower gardens and trash cans, which is reason enough to keep your cat safely inside and out of harm's way.

Introducing a Cat to Other Pets

If you already have an adult cat or a dog, bringing a new kitten into their territory must be managed thoughtfully and carefully. Before exposing any newcomer to your resident cat(s), have the new cat checked by a veterinarian and tested for parasites and contagious diseases, especially feline leukemia virus (FeLV) and feline immune deficiency virus (FIV).

While awaiting the test results, keep the new arrival isolated from your other pets, in a separate room or in a cage. This also allows time for the house smell to settle on the newcomer, which may help make the introductions less threatening. After a few days, remove the new cat from its separate quarters for a while and let the resident pets go in and sniff the new scent. When the time seems right, allow the resident pets to see and sniff the newcomer, but supervise all contact for the first few weeks. Keep dogs on a leash during these first meetings so they won't chase and frighten the newcomer. Gradually increase the exposure time until the pets seem to settle down and become acquainted.

Although it's usually easier to introduce a kitten, rather than a grown cat, into a home that already has a feline, don't be dismayed if it takes as long as a month for the animals to accept each other and become friends. Cats are territorial creatures, and adding a newcomer to the environment means that new boundaries must be set. In time, the tension usually disappears; however, cats, like people, are individuals, and occasionally two turn out to be simply incompatible. Most shelters and breeders will agree to take back an animal if things don't work out in the new home, but just in case, always make sure your purchase or adoption agreement clearly states the terms of a return policy.

Dogs: Before introducing a cat or kitten to a household with a grown

dog, you need to consider many factors, such as the size and temperament of the dog, how the dog has been trained, and whether the dog is already a confirmed cat chaser. Cats and dogs that have been raised together since they were kittens and puppies generally get along well. Puppies raised around cats learn to recognize them as friends or members of their pack. Kittens raised around cat-friendly canines grow up without learning to fear them. However, a main concern with such youngsters growing up together is preventing the two from harming each other unintentionally during play sessions that get too rough. For example, a large, rambunctious puppy can kill a small kitten without meaning to. Supervision and controlled encounters are a must until the kitten is big enough to escape the puppy or dog's unwanted atten-

tions, or until the two learn their limits around each other.

Birds and small mammals: If you have rabbits, guinea pigs, birds, or other small pets, it's possible to achieve harmony among different species as long as you provide secure, separate living quarters for all and supervise any direct contact. Large pet birds, such as parrots, can hurt a small kitten with their strong beaks and talons. While there have been reports of cats and pet birds striking up unusual friendships, it is never wise to leave an adult cat alone with uncaged birds or small animals of prey. Cats are natural predators, and it is neither fair nor reasonable to expect them to ignore or control their instincts under such circumstances.

Ferrets: Because of their razor-sharp teeth, ferrets can pose more of a danger to cats, particularly kittens, rather than the other way around. However, as long as careful, gradual introductions are made, and close supervision is maintained when needed, it is possible for the two species to become accustomed to one another and eventually grow into playmates.

Fish and reptiles: Cats are fascinated by swimming fish, so if you have an aquarium, cover it with a lighting hood, so your cat won't be tempted to go fishing or swimming. Some large pet snakes, such as boa constrictors, can be hazardous to have around kittens and any other small mammals that might be mistaken for a meal and swallowed. If you keep snakes, secure them

safely in a separate area of the house, and make sure that exploring cats cannot accidentally overturn the snake containers.

Cats and Kids

Children find kittens irresistible, but they have to be taught how to handle them properly. Not only can a child injure a fragile kitten, but an animal frightened or annoyed by a child's unintentional roughness may defend itself by scratching or biting the child. To avoid such mishaps, teach your child that pets are not animated toys, and supervise all physical contact between small children and pets. If the child pulls on a cat's tail or ears, remove his hand and show him how to gently stroke the animal's fur. Explain to your child that loud screams and sudden movements may frighten the cat. Show your child where cats like to be stroked most—under the chin, behind the ears, and on the neck and back. Explain that some cats do not like to be stroked on their stomachs and rumps, while others will tolerate it from people they know well and trust. Teach your child how to properly pick up and hold a cat.

How to pick up a cat: The proper way to pick up a cat is to put one hand under the chest behind the forelegs and the other hand under the rump to support the rear legs and body. Cradle the cat in your arms against your chest. Your cat will let you know when he wants down.

Although mother cats carry their kittens by the scruff of the neck, this method is not recommended. Carrying by the neck scruff can injure an adult cat if not done properly and should be reserved for emergency restraint. Even then, care must be taken to fully support the cat's rear legs and body weight with the other hand. Allowing the cat's full weight to dangle without such support can seriously injure those neck and back muscles. Likewise, never lift a cat by the ears or front paws.

Cats and Babies

Couples planning a family often ask whether they can keep their cat and still have a baby. We've all heard that ridiculous old wives' tale about cats sucking the breath from infants. Certainly, it's wise not to allow your cat to have unsupervised access to an infant, not because there's any truth to silly old wives' tales, but because a baby's screams, cries, or jerky movements may frighten the cat and result in accidental scratching or biting. If necessary, install a screen door at the nursery entrance. Also, to keep cats out of the cradle, consider buying a mesh crib tent. Baby supply stores sell these as well as cat nets that cover playpens and strollers.

Toxoplasmosis deserves a mention here, because it's one of those scary reasons well-meaning people bring up to convince mothers-to-be that their cats must go before a new baby comes. If you're planning to have a baby, get the facts first from your obstetrician and veterinarian. Tests are available to detect the disease, which is caused by a protozoan. Studies indicate that most people already have a degree of immunity to the disease, but if a pregnant woman is exposed to it for the first time, birth defects can occur.

Of course, a cat has to acquire the disease first, before he can pass it on to a human being. Cats get the disease by eating infected birds, rodents, or raw meat, then they shed the eggs in their feces. Humans can get the disease by handling soil or litter contaminated by the feces of an infected cat. But the majority of cases in humans are not the result of contact with cats, but instead, can be traced to people eating undercooked meat.

Cats can be tested for the disease, and if found to be free of the infection, there's no cause for worry. If your cat never roams outdoors, never hunts, eats prepackaged commercial pet foods and is never fed raw or undercooked meat, the chances of him ever acquiring the disease are virtually nonexistent.

If you become pregnant or plan to, discuss this important issue with your doctor. When you know the facts and observe sensible precautions—such as thoroughly cooking all meats before eating, washing your hands after handling raw meats, and wearing gloves when gardening or cleaning the cat box—there's generally no need whatsoever to give up your cat if you're going to have a baby.

As a general health precaution, keep indoor litter boxes and pet feeding bowls out of a crawling child's range. And cover children's outdoor sandboxes when not in use, so that free-roaming cats won't mistake them for oversized litter boxes.

Sometimes a cat may urinate on a baby's bedding or other items, *marking* them as part of his territory. Restricting access to the nursery will help prevent this normal but undesirable behavior. Spaying and neutering also tend to curb marking behaviors in cats (see page 157 for more on territorial marking).

Finally, to reduce accidental scratches, trim your cat's claws regularly. And of course, keeping your cat in good health, keeping his shots up-to-date and making sure he remains free of fleas, ticks, and other parasites, reduces the risk of dis-ease transmission to yourself and your family. In other words, contrary to what those old wives' tales imply, cats and babies can coexist peaceably as long as you use some common-sense precautions.

Cat Care While You're Away

When planning a vacation, ask a trusted friend or neighbor to look in on your cat, or consider hiring a pet-sitter to care for your pet while you're away. Leaving your cat in his normal environment is less traumatic than boarding him in unfamiliar surroundings at a kennel or a veterinarian's office. However, deviation from the normal household routine upsets some animals and may result in behavior problems, such as house-

soiling. If your cat is subject to this behavior, he may be better off at a boarding facility, where he can be supervised. To ease your cat's separation anxiety, leave something with your scent on it, such as an unwashed T-shirt or house slipper, to comfort the cat while you're away.

If you decide to use a professional pet-sitter or boarding kennel, ask friends for recommendations, and check out the operator's references and business credentials. Inspect a boarding facility's premises for cleanliness beforehand, and ask about provisions for your cat's security and comfort. Select a kennel that houses cats in an area separate from dogs. A reputable kennel will require pets to be free of fleas and will also ask for proof that animals are up-to-date on all inoculations.

Whatever arrangements you choose to make, leave an itinerary of where you will be and how you can be reached. Also, be sure to leave your veterinarian's telephone number with the person tending to your cat. One obvious advantage of boarding your cat at a veterinary hospital is that medically trained personnel are on hand to observe and handle any emergency illness your cat may experience while you're away.

Even if you're going to be away for several hours and leave out enough food and water in self-feeders for your cat, let someone know where you're going and when you'll be back. That person also should have a key to your home and permission to enter and look after your

cat in case you're involved in an accident that delays your return.

Pet Identification

Because cats kept indoors occasionally escape and get lost in unfamiliar territory, it's a good idea to have some kind of pet identification on your cat. Even when a lost pet is picked up and placed in an animal shelter, he typically has little chance of being reunited with his original owner, unless he is wearing some form of identification. For this reason, and because some people steal pets for resale, your cat is safer if he wears some sort of identification. While this simple precaution may not prevent your cat from being lost or stolen, a permanent ID may enhance his chances of recovery. Most shelters look for tattoos and other forms of pet ID.

Tattooing: A painless procedure provided by many veterinarians, tattooing involves inking the owner's Social Security number or a special code on the rear inner thigh. Avoid tattooing inside the earflap, as ears can be cut off. For best results, register the tattoo with a nationwide pet protection service that has a 24-hour hotline for tracing the number and finding the owner, no matter where the cat is found. The veterinarian who does the tattooing can recommend an appropriate registry.

Collars and tags: These can be lost or removed, but they are better than nothing. A suitable cat collar should have a stretch elastic or a breakaway section, so the animal can escape without choking if the collar snags on a tree branch or other object.

Like collars, ear tags embedded in the ear like a tiny earring are better than no ID at all, but they, too, can be cut off, ear and all, by unscrupulous pet thieves.

Microchips: Animal shelters in many areas are using microchip technology to reunite lost pets with their owners. To use such an ID system, the owner has a veterinarian inject a tiny microchip under the skin between the cat's shoulder blades. The chip reflects radio waves emitted by a handheld scanner, which reads the chip's code number. The owner then registers the code number in a computer database for tracking. Ask your veterinarian if such a system is available in your area.

When Things Don't Work Out

Sometimes, despite your best efforts and planning, you may acquire a cat that just doesn't adjust well to your home or to other pets. If you recently purchased or adopted the cat, you may be able to take the animal back to the breeder, pet store, or shelter.

In addition, circumstances can arise in everyone's life that leave no alternative but to part with pets. Responsible pet owners will always try to find a good home for their cat first, before surrendering him to a shelter for adoption. Perhaps a relative, friend, or neighbor will adopt the cat. If the cat has never been accustomed to being outside, make sure you place the animal with someone who wants an indoor pet.

If you can't find someone to take your cat, tack up a notice on the bulletin board where you work or at your veterinarian's office. Or advertise your cat in the classified section of your local newspaper. When doing so, however, avoid the *Free to Good Home* come-on. Instead, attach a nominal fee to your cat's head, even if it's as little as $10 or so. People tend to place greater value on something they pay for, even when the price is small.

Chapter Four

Feeding Your Cat: Feline Nutrition Basics

The Carnivorous Cat

The basis of any good cat food is meat, or animal protein. In fact, the scientific community often refers to cats as *obligate* carnivores, meaning that they must eat meat to stay healthy. This does not mean, however, that an all-meat or all-fish diet is healthier for them than a diet that simply contains sufficient meat. Quite the opposite is true; cats also require important nutrients that come from plant sources. Under natural conditions, feral cats generally consume most or all of the body parts of their small mammal prey, including any plant material that happens to remain in the stomach. This material provides important nutrients, such as fiber, calcium, and B vitamins, generally not found in adequate amounts in an all-meat diet. While ground, grilled, or chopped mouse in a can may be the most natural cat food, the chances of such a product going over well with the human consumer who has to buy it are nil. Because pet food manufacturers must satisfy two consumers—the cat and the owner—they historically have used culturally accepted foodstuffs as protein sources—fish, poultry, beef—and added cereals, grains, and synthetic vitamins and minerals, as necessary, to achieve the recommended nutrient balance established by scientific research.

While plant source nutrients are beneficial, it is important to know that cats cannot thrive on a vegetar-

ian diet. Although humans may elect to be vegetarians for health or moral reasons, nature intended for cats to be predatory carnivores. Having evolved as such, cats require much more protein than either humans or dogs, and while some of that protein can come from plant sources, a certain amount must come from animal sources. Cats simply cannot remain healthy for long on foods made solely from plant sources.

Commercial Cat Foods

Commercial cat foods today are researched and formulated to provide enough animal protein and other essential nutrients needed for good feline health. The Association of American Feed Control Officials (AAFCO) has established cat food nutrient profiles, testing protocols, and labeling regulations for the pet food industry to follow. The major pet food manufacturers use AAFCO's nutrient profiles and testing protocols as the standard for formulating and substantiating the nutrient content of their products.

Walk down any grocery store pet food aisle, and you'll find a large array of cat food products to select from. While the sheer number of choices may confuse and overwhelm some consumers, having so many choices available on the market is a big plus for pet owners. The variety and competition make it rela-

tively easy to find good products that your cat will relish and that will be convenient for you to serve.

Despite the numerous products available, commercial pet foods come in three basic types: dry, canned, and semimoist (also called soft-dry). Each type comes in a variety of flavors as well. While there's no reason to complicate the selection process, there are some advantages and disadvantages of each type of food to consider before you settle on a favorite.

Dry Foods

Dry foods are generally less expensive to buy and more convenient to serve. They are not as smelly as canned foods, and they can be left out all day without spoiling for cats to nibble *ad libitum* or at will. Called free-choice feeding, this is the method most often recommended in the product-feeding guidelines on a dry food package label.

However, owners sometimes make the mistake of leaving out too much dry food, encouraging their cats to overeat and grow fat. Instead of putting out bulk amounts of dry food that could last for several days, it is best to carefully measure out each meal or each day's portion, using the product feeding recommendations as a guide. By leaving out only controlled portions of dry food for free-choice nibbling, you are less likely to end up with an obese cat.

Dry foods also may benefit cats by promoting better dental health.

Although this issue has been widely debated, it is generally believed that the hard chewing action required with dry foods helps scour the teeth and gums and therefore aids in controlling ugly tartar buildup that can lead to gum disease and tooth loss. Because cats tend to swallow their food almost whole, the benefits of such chewing action are probably minimal at best. Therefore, exclusively feeding dry foods should not be considered a substitute for routine dental care (see page 128).

Canned Foods

Canned foods are usually more expensive than dry foods. They contain more moisture than either dry or semimoist foods, making them a better choice for cats that need more water due to some medical condition, such as kidney disease. For cats that have missing teeth or sore gums due to dental disease, canned foods are also ideal because they require virtually no chewing.

Finicky eaters also seem to prefer canned foods and will often select them over dry foods because most canned foods apparently taste better to the feline consumer. Canned foods typically contain more protein and fat than either dry or semimoist foods, which makes them generally more palatable to the feline taste buds.

Single-serving cans, although more expensive, result in less waste, because many cats will refuse to eat canned food after it has been refrigerated. Having evolved as predators,

cats prefer their food warm, at the average body temperature of small prey animals or, at least, at normal room temperature. So always warm refrigerated leftovers before serving.

Canned foods will spoil quickly and attract insects if left out too long, so free-choice feeding is not an option with this type. To avoid spoilage and odors, take up any uneaten portions of canned food as soon as the cat finishes eating.

Semimoist Foods

Semimoist foods typically come in soft-dry nuggets packaged in foil-lined wrappers or bags. These food products attempt to combine some benefits of the dry and canned types, making them an attractive, middle-of-the-road choice for the human consumer to use. Semimoist foods contain more moisture than dry foods, but they lack the odors of canned foods that human consumers so often find offensive. Also, like dry rations, semimoist foods can be left out and fed free-choice without spoiling. Unlike dry foods, however, semimoist products are too soft to help reduce dental tartar. The convenience packaging is a major advantage, because the single-serving foil pouches take the guesswork out of controlled-portion feeding.

Popular Versus Premium Brands

Aside from the basic food types, cat foods are also packaged and marketed according to whether they are generic (economy brands), popular (supermarket), or premium brands.

Economy brands: While the cheaper generic foods, which are typically sold under a private label or store name, tend to be lower in quality and use poorer-grade ingredients, this is not always true. Sometimes it is cheaper for a manufacturer to simply stick a generic label on a popular brand and market it under a different name without changing the formula. Before choosing a generic brand, however, you should contact the manufacturer and thoroughly research the product ingredients. In general, you get what you pay for. Comparative studies have shown that some generic brands use poorer-grade ingredients, have lower energy values, and are less digestible. An animal has to eat more of a poorly digestible food to extract adequate nutrient value from the contents. In terms of quantity consumed, this can actually cost you more if you have to feed your cat more.

Popular or supermarket brands: These are the nationally advertised name-brand products sold in supermarkets, that people are most familiar with. They cost more than generic brands, but usually not as much as the premium or super-premium brands sold primarily through pet supply stores. Compared to some economy brands, popular brands tend to contain better-quality ingredients and are more digestible. These formulas are often well researched and designed to meet the nutritional needs of the average cat at specified life stages.

Premium brands: There is no industry-regulated definition for what a *premium* or a *super-premium* product should be, and no higher nutritional standard that premium pet foods must adhere to. These words are simply descriptive marketing tools. Other than price, some popular and premium brands may differ very little. The general assumption is, however, that premium foods contain higher-quality ingredients and remain stable in their makeup, whereas popular brands are more likely to change recipe ingredients

according to the current market cost and availability of those ingredients.

Premium products also are often marketed as being more digestible and energy dense, which means that a smaller amount is required per serving to provide the necessary nutrients. Greater digestibility means less waste, which translates to smaller stool volume in the litter box. One way to determine how well your cat seems to be digesting a particular food is to note how much is coming out the other end. Large, bulky stools indicate poor digestibility.

Another general assumption about premium brands is that the product research behind premium brands is more substantial. However, many well-known popular brands are also backed by extensive research and years of experience on the part of the manufacturer.

Therapeutic diets: These are often called prescription diets and also are available through veterinarians for cats with special needs.

These foods are formulated and dispensed by veterinarians specifically for certain health conditions, such as heart disease, kidney disease, intestinal disorders, or obesity (see Veterinary-dispensed Weight-loss Diets, page 101). Because therapeutic diets are designed for the medical management of cats with specific needs, these special foods should not be fed to healthy cats in your household. If you have a cat that requires a special diet, feed him separately from your other cats.

The Nutrients Cats Need

To be nutritionally complete and balanced, a cat food designed to be fed to a feline every day as the animal's staple diet must contain the proper amounts of plant and animal protein, plus the right mixture of amino acids, carbohydrates, fiber, fats, vitamins, and minerals.

Amino Acids

There are more than 20 amino acids. They are important chemical components cats need to synthesize body proteins. Many experts describe them as the building blocks of protein, since protein is made up of amino acids, and without them, the feline body cannot effectively use the food it consumes. Amino acids are divided into two groups: essential and nonessential. The cat's body can manufacture nonessential amino acids in sufficient amounts to maintain good health, but essential amino acids must come from the diet because cats cannot manufacture them on their own. Essential amino acids required by cats include:

• Arginine
• Histidine
• Isoleucine
• Leucine
• Lysine
• Methionine
• Phenylalanine
• Taurine
• Threonine
• Tryptophan
• Valine

One or more of these essential amino acids may be listed as an additive on a cat food label. Those not listed on the label occur naturally in the cat food ingredients. Without sufficient amounts of these essential amino acids in the diet, cats cannot remain healthy. Kittens can experience stunted growth if their diets lack essential amino acids. Symptoms of an amino acid or protein deficiency may include weight loss, appetite loss, overall poor condition, muscle spasms, drooling, cataracts, and incoordination.

Arginine helps convert ammonia, a toxic by-product of protein metabolism, into urea so that it can be safely excreted from the body in the urine. Because cats cannot manufacture sufficient amounts of arginine in their livers, they must obtain this essential amino acid from their diets; otherwise, a deficiency could cause a dangerous buildup of ammonia in the blood. Fortunately, this condition rarely occurs in cats fed complete and balanced commercial diets. However, cats may be put at risk of a deficiency when allowed to subsist solely on people food and table scraps, or when exclusively fed a homemade diet that has not been recommended or supervised by a veterinarian with training in animal nutrition.

Taurine is an essential nutrient for felines. Cats are the only known mammals that cannot manufacture enough taurine on their own for good health. Sufficient amounts must be supplied in the feline diet. Taurine deficiency can cause dilated cardiomyopathy, which is a heart disease, and central retinal degeneration, which is an eye problem that can lead to blindness. Years ago, when taurine deficiency was first linked to these heart and eye problems in cats, responsible pet food manufacturers began adding more of this essential nutrient to their products. Since then, reported cases of dilated cardiomyopathy have declined dramatically. Today, high-quality, complete and balanced cat foods contain enough taurine to help ensure good health. Canned cat foods typically have more taurine added to their formulas than do dry foods, because the canning process appears to affect taurine availability.

Carbohydrates

Carbohydrates are starches, sugars, cereals, and grain fibers. Common sources in cat foods typically include processed rice, soy, corn, wheat, barley, oats, and corn gluten meal. Carbohydrates are used in commercial cat foods as important sources of energy and fiber. They break down into glucose, a simple sugar that provides energy to the body's cells. Although carbohydrate requirements have not been established for cats, the average dry commercial cat foods contain about 40 percent carbohydrates, most of which comes from cereals and grains. The grinding, flaking, and cooking methods used to process these cereal grains tend to improve the food's taste and digestibility, according to industry experts.

Fiber

The fiber content of complex carbohydrates provides bulk, also called roughage, which helps regulate the movement of food through the cat's intestines. Fiber content in pet food is reported on the label as *crude fiber,* which is a rough estimate at best. (The term *crude* does not refer to the quality of the ingredient, but rather is a method of measuring the amount.) Common fiber sources in pet foods include guar gum, wheat bran, corn, and beans. The various chemical components of fiber are often referred to as cellulose, lignin, pectin, gum, or mucilage.

The effects of dietary fiber vary with the type of fiber present and with the way it's processed. Different types of fiber take up more or less water in the intestinal tract, thereby changing the speed at which food passes through the gut. This particular property makes fiber an important tool in the treatment of constipation or chronic diarrhea.

The amount of fiber fed is also important. Too much fiber in the diet can cause excessive gas, loose stools, or increased stool volume. The often-stated rule of thumb is all too true: "More fiber in, more feces out." In fact, foods containing too much poor-quality fiber can actually

have a negative impact on feline health by slowing the absorption and hampering the digestibility of vital nutrients.

But specially designed, good-quality, high-fiber foods can be beneficial in the treatment of certain disorders, such as obesity, diabetes, and bowel disease. Because they are often used to manage medical conditions, these special diets are generally sold through veterinarians. Fiber is also thought to provide some protection against certain cancer-causing toxins by binding with them and preventing their absorption into the bloodstream.

Fat

Dietary fats, also called *lipids,* provide more calories and concentrated energy than carbohydrates or proteins. They are either saturated or unsaturated. Saturated fats are solid

at room temperature; unsaturated fats are liquid. Two fatty acids are essential to cats: linoleic acid and arachidonic acid. Linoleic acid is available in vegetable oils, whereas arachidonic acid is available to cats only from animal fat. Other animals can convert linoleic acid to arachidonic acid, but cats cannot. They must derive the latter substance from animal sources, which is another reason why cats must have meat in their diets.

Just as a higher fat content can make food taste better to humans, the same is true for cats. In fact, manufacturers may add more fat and protein to some foods just to enhance the taste, or palatability. As expected, such foods are also usually higher in calories, since fats contain more than twice the calories of protein or carbohydrates. Of course, cats cannot tell how many fats and calories are in their food. They simply eat what tastes good to them, and they eat until they feel full and satisfied.

But unless a cat is overweight, health-conscious humans really need not worry about their cats' fat consumption. For one thing, fats help make your cat's coat shiny and healthy looking. Also, feline fat requirements differ vastly from ours. Cats readily tolerate higher levels of fat in their daily diet than humans. In fact, cats seem to have evolved with a much more efficient way of metabolizing and handling cholesterol, a type of lipid well known for the health complications it can cause in humans when present in too-high

amounts. Prepared pet foods often contain a lot of beef tallow, which is rich in saturated fats, yet cats don't seem to develop atherosclerosis and related coronary artery disease as people do. The reason for this may be because cats have a lot more of the good cholesterol than the bad. Good cholesterol, or high-density lipoproteins (HDL), carry cholesterol out of the body's tissues to the liver for disposal. Bad cholesterol, or low-density lipoproteins (LDL), carry cholesterol to the body tissues. In cats, the ratio of good to bad, or HDL to LDL, is 4 to 1; in humans the ratio is reverse. Why cats are able to maintain higher levels of HDL than LDL is not well understood.

Fats not only enhance the taste of cat food, but are important carriers of fat-soluble vitamins. Fat sources in the feline diet may include fish oil, soybean oil, wheat germ oil, and animal fat. As mentioned previously, fats also help maintain a healthy skin and hair coat. Symptoms of essential fatty acid deficiency include a dull coat, flaking skin, hair loss, crusty sores, frequent illness, listlessness, and overall poor condition. Studies show that linoleic acid deficiency can impair growth and reproduction and affect the kidneys, connective tissues, and red blood cells.

Protein

Protein promotes growth and tissue repair and sustains the immune system in all mammals. Primary sources of protein include the lean muscle meats, while secondary sources include whole cereal grains and soybean meal. Cats need protein for energy. Unlike humans, cats cannot use carbohydrates or fats in place of protein to supply all of their calories and energy needs. Because cats cannot store excess protein, they must consume the required amount daily from their food.

To the cat, animal protein sources, such as beef, lamb, chicken, fish meal, or turkey, are especially important, because they contain most or all of the essential amino acids. As important as protein and meat are to the cat, too much is likely to be just as harmful as too little; however, some owners mistakenly believe that more meat is better for their carnivorous pets and will lavish them with exclusive diets of liver, fish, and beef, when in fact, an all-meat or all-fish diet can lead to certain deficiency symptoms and disorders (see page 91). These deficiencies do not necessarily stem from an excess of protein, but rather from an improper balance of calcium and other important minerals and vitamins. Meat alone is simply not a balanced meal and cannot provide the cat with all of the required nutrients.

To avoid such deficiencies, choose only complete and balanced cat foods. These contain all the protein and other nutrients your cat needs. For variety, these foods come in a wide selection of protein sources, from different kinds of fish, to poultry, to lamb and other meats, to meat by-products. Meat by-products are simply animal parts and cuts of meat not generally used for human consumption, such as the heart, brain, tongue, stomach, and so on. Dry foods often are sprayed with a protein *digest,* which is a liquefied, chemically predigested meat added primarily to enhance palatability.

The protein quality and digestibility are even more important than the quantity. The term *digestibility* refers to how much of the protein present in a food can actually be absorbed and used for energy by the animal that eats it. The amount that can't be used is excreted as waste. Two different products may list the same percentage of protein on their packages, but controlled feeding studies may reveal very different levels of digestibility. In general, higher-quality, premium cat foods provide greater protein digestibility.

Vitamins

Most vitamins cannot be manufactured internally and must be obtained from the diet; however, cats can manufacture their own vitamin C and K. Felines have an especially high requirement for the B complex vitamins—thiamine, riboflavin, niacin, biotin, and so forth—

Water-Soluble Vitamins and What They Do to Keep Your Cat Healthy

Vitamin	Function
B1 (also called *thiamine*)	Carbohydrate metabolism, normal neurologic function
B2 *(riboflavin)*	Cellular growth; normal vision; healthy skin
B6 *(pyridoxine)*	Protein and amino acid metabolism; kidney and urinary tract health
Niacin	Produces biochemical reactions that help the body use all major nutrients
Pantothenic acid	Carbohydrate, fat, and amino acid metabolism
Folacin *(folic acid)*	Normal growth and red blood cell production
Biotin	Necessary for certain biochemical reactions during metabolism; healthy skin
B12 *(cyanocobalamin)*	Fat and carbohydrate metabolism
Choline	Moves fat from the liver and synthesizes the amino acid methionine
Vitamin C *(ascorbic acid)*	Acts as an antioxidant; aids in cell repair

Fat-Soluble Vitamins and What They Do to Keep Your Cat Healthy

Vitamin	Function
Vitamin A *(retinol)*	Healthy vision; cell membrane regulation; growth
Vitamin D *(ergocalciferol, cholecalciferol)*	Calcium and phosphorus metabolism; bone growth
Vitamin E *(tocopherol)*	Antioxidant properties; aids normal reproduction
Vitamin K *(menadione in synthetic form)*	Aids in normal blood clotting

particularly during periods of stress, illness, growth, or lactation. But as long as the cat owner feeds a complete and balanced cat food, vitamin supplements are rarely necessary and should not be given, unless recommended by a veterinarian. In fact, overdoses of certain vitamins, such as A and D, can be toxic to cats.

Sensitive to heat, light, moisture, and rancidity, vitamins are easily destroyed if food isn't prepared, packaged, and stored properly. Vitamin sources in cat foods may be listed on the label as brewer's yeast (B complex), menadione (vitamin K), choline, lecithin, and folic acid, among others.

Vitamins are classified as either fat-soluble or water-soluble. Fat-soluble vitamins require the presence of fat in the diet for proper absorption to take place; water-soluble vitamins depend on adequate water for that purpose. Like many minerals, vitamins work together and with other nutrients to perform their necessary functions, which is why adding unwarranted supplements to the diet can upset this delicate balance and cause detrimental side effects.

Antioxidants

Vitamin E, sometimes listed as *tocopheral* on a cat food label, and the mineral selenium are good examples of nutrients that work together to act as an antioxidant. Antioxidants, present in certain foods, function at the cellular level to protect the body against cell damage from too many *free radicals.* Free radicals are unstable oxygen molecules, produced during normal body metabolism, that can steal electrons from stable molecules, triggering potentially detrimental chemical changes called oxidation. Antioxidants exist to keep these renegade free radicals in check, thereby minimizing cell damage. Although an important nutrient for its antioxidant properties with vitamin E, selenium is known to be toxic to many animals at higher than the trace levels normally found in the body. The other vitamins and what they are important for in good feline health are listed in the chart on page 69.

Minerals

Cats need certain minerals to help synthesize vitamins, produce hormones, promote normal bone growth, transport oxygen in the blood, maintain fluid and electrolyte balance, and aid in muscle and nerve functions. For good health, cats need proper amounts of calcium, phosphorus, sodium, chloride, iron, potassium, magnesium, iodine, copper, zinc, manganese, and selenium. To a lesser extent, cats also seem to require, as do some other animals, the trace minerals sulfur, fluorine, chromium, tin, silicon, nickel, molybdenum, and vanadium. The chart on page 71 lists the various minerals and explains why they are important for your cat's health.

Some minerals occur naturally in the ingredients that make up cat

Minerals and What They Do to Keep Your Cat Healthy

Mineral	Function
Calcium (Ca)	Important for strong bones and teeth, normal blood clotting, nerve transmission
Phosphorus (P)	Important for normal bone development
Sodium (Na)	Important for normal metabolism, fluid regulation, transfer of nutrients to cells
Chloride (Cl)	Important for normal metabolism, formation of hydrochloric acid in the stomach
Potassium (K)	Maintains fluid balance and proper nerve, enzyme, immune system functions
Magnesium (Mg)	Component of muscle and bone; influences enzymatic reactions
Iron (Fe)	Helps form hemoglobin, the oxygen-carrying component of red blood cells
Zinc (Zn)	Activates important enzymes and aids normal protein metabolism
Copper (Cu)	Helps prevent anemia, important for iron metabolism and connective tissue
Manganese (Mn)	Important for reproduction and proper bone formation, activates enzymes
Selenium (Se)	Works with vitamin E to act as an antioxidant in the body
Cobalt (Co)	Component of vitamin B12, which is critical to certain metabolic functions
Iodine (I)	Aids in production of thyroid hormones by the thyroid gland

food, and therefore, may not appear on the cat food label. Minerals added to supplement the ingredient mix may be listed on a label as bone meal (phosphorus, calcium), sodium (salt), cobalt carbonate, phosphoric acid, manganese sulfate, potassium iodide, zinc sulfate, and ferrous sulfate (iron), among others.

Minerals and Urinary Tract Health

Magnesium is just one of several dietary constituents blamed in the past as a contributing factor in feline urologic syndrome or FUS. Today, most veterinarians refer to this condition as FLUTD or LUTD, which stands for feline lower urinary tract disease, an umbrella term for related disorders. It is a potentially life-threatening condition caused by tiny mineral crystals that form in the urinary tract, leading to painful irritation and sometimes serious blockages. Warning signs include visiting the litter box frequently, urinating in unusual places, straining to urinate, and passing blood-tinged urine.

Acid-base balance: While studies clearly implicate a connection between FLUTD and high magnesium levels in the feline diet, leading many laymen to believe that this essential nutrient is bad, current findings indicate that the overall mineral composition of cat food, rather than an excess of any single ingredient, plays a greater role in maintaining the body's acid-base balance than was previously understood. The acid-base conditions determine whether the urine pH stays within normal acidic ranges or becomes too alkaline. The higher (more alkaline) the urine pH, the more favorable the conditions for mineral crystals to form in the urinary tract, while at the lower levels (more acidic), the acid urine helps dissolve these struvite waste crystals or prevent them from forming in the first place. Carnivores typically produce an acid urine; plant-eating animals tend to produce an alkaline urine.

Without attention to the overall mineral composition, cat foods with a high vegetable or cereal content can cause the cat to produce an alkaline urine. For this reason, allowing cats to nibble free-choice on dry foods throughout the day was once discouraged because it was thought that this practice predisposed cats to FLUTD. This opinion began to change, however, after responsible pet food manufacturers, armed with the latest scientific knowledge, started adding acidifying ingredients to their formulas to help keep urine pH within safely acidic ranges. Today, most commercial cat foods, including dry foods, are believed to contain enough acidifying ingredients to help maintain normal pH balance, and free-choice feeding is now the generally recommended feeding method for most dry foods.

Magnesium content: While urinary acidity is the most important

factor in feline lower urinary tract disease, magnesium content in cat food remains a secondary concern, enough to warrant restricting dietary levels when managing an individual's recurrent bouts of FLUTD. So, what about commercial diets that help maintain urinary tract health, the ones bearing label claims of *low magnesium, reduces urinary pH, or helps maintain urinary tract health?* Beyond these permissible statements, cat food manufacturers cannot claim that their products treat or prevent FLUTD, or any other disease, without approval from the Food and Drug Administration, because to do so would be touting the diet as a drug.

Struvite stones: With the addition of acidifying ingredients to commercial cat foods, researchers have noted a decrease in struvite stones in cats. But the news isn't all good. Experts also report a coinciding increase in similar stones composed of a different material, calcium oxalate. The obvious conclusion is that the recomposition of commercial diets fed to cats is at least partly responsible for both changes.

What does all this mean? While studies clearly suggest that restricting magnesium and maintaining a slightly acidic urine may help prevent struvite-related urethral obstructions, such a diet is certainly not considered a cure-all for all cats, particularly if it has the potential to cause other problems. And while the link between diet and urinary tract disease is still being studied, the best advice is simply to consult your veterinarian before starting your cat on any special diet. Furthermore, if you suspect your cat may have a urinary tract problem, seek veterinary attention immediately. Dietary management may be only part of the necessary treatment.

Preservatives and Other Additives

Many health-conscious pet owners harbor concerns about the preservatives and additives used in cat foods. Although many preservatives have little or no nutritional value, they are necessary components of cat food, because they prevent spoilage and extend the shelf life of products. They serve as antimicrobials or antioxidants, or both. As an antimicrobial, preservatives prevent the growth of harmful molds, yeasts, and bacteria in foods. As an antioxidant, preservatives prevent fats from becoming rancid. They do this by suppressing the reaction called oxidation that occurs when food combines with oxygen in the presence of light, heat, and some metals.

Common Chemical Preservatives

• BHA (butylated hydroxyanisole), BHT (butylated hydroxytoluene), and ethoxyquin are common chemical preservatives added to fats in pet foods to prevent rancidity.
• Vitamin E (tocopherol) is a natural antioxidant widely used as a preservative to prevent fat rancidity. Rancid fats ruin the taste of the food and give off an unpleasant odor so that the cat is reluctant to eat. Rancidity can also damage essential amino

acids and destroy important fat-soluble vitamins contained in the food. Not only does the food become unpleasant and unfit for consumption, it may even become toxic to the pet.
• The antioxidant ethoxyquin is used in small amounts as a preservative in some pet foods. Besides preventing fat rancidity, studies indicate that the chemical may also protect against the poisonous effects of mold-induced mycotoxins, which can be a problem in some preservative-free foods. According to the Food and Drug Administration's Center for Veterinary Medicine (FDA-CVM), manufacturers are supposed to declare ethoxyquin on the label if a pet food contains it, regardless of whether they add the chemical directly or whether the ingredients they used came with the substance already included.

Because of its classification as a chemical for agricultural use, ethoxyquin has been the subject of much controversy. Although consumers have raised concerns about ethoxyquin allegedly causing cancer, thyroid disorders, reproductive failures, and other problems, repeated tests have failed to reveal any significant health risks associated with the amounts of ethoxyquin allowed in pet foods. In response to these consumer concerns, however, many pet food manufacturers have replaced ethoxyquin with the natural preservatives, vitamin E (tocopherols) and vitamin C (ascorbic acid). However, products preserved with the latter two substances tend to have a somewhat shorter shelf life.

• Another preservative has been removed from cat foods due to health concerns. When first introduced, semimoist foods contained propylene glycol, an ingredient used in cosmetics and alcoholic beverages. (Propylene glycol is also the main ingredient in safer antifreeze brands, making them less toxic than traditional antifreeze brands, see page 48.) The substance acted primarily as a humectant, preserving the moisture retention in the soft-dry foods, but when the chemical was implicated in causing red blood cell damage in cats, its use in cat foods was discontinued. Today, the more common preservatives used in semimoist foods to prevent mold and bacterial growth include sorbic acid and potassium sorbate. Glycerin is added as a humectant.

Other additives may provide artificial coloring or flavoring or act as vitamin and mineral sources. All chemical preservatives and nonnutritive additives must be approved by the Food and Drug Administration (FDA) for use in pet foods. Also, any drug used in pet foods is also subject to FDA approval. To help ensure that they are harmless to pets, such substances must undergo required testing and meet certain criteria before approval for use is granted.

Artificial Colors

In general, artificial colors used in cat foods are the same ones approved for use in human foods. When used, colors are added for the human consumer's benefit rather than the cat's. Cats, of course, don't care what color their food is, as long as it tastes good, but for humans, these additives give products a more uniform, attractive appearance than the natural ingredients would provide in their natural state. Colors also help the human consumer differentiate between flavors in multiflavored foods. Because artificial colors have no nutritive value, foods without coloring, which are typically a flat, incon-

sistent gray or brown in appearance, are no more or less nutritious than identical products enhanced with colors. If you have expensive rugs and carpets in your home, you may want to consider avoiding foods with artificial colors, as some coloring agents can leave stains if the cat vomits his food. The following color additives have at one time or another been used in pet foods: caramel, titanium dioxide, Red No. 40, Red No. 3, Yellow No. 5, Yellow No. 6, Blue No. 1, and Blue No. 2.

Flavoring Agents

Flavoring agents provide a convenient way to make products more palatable to cats. Flavorings are either artificial ingredients with long chemical names, or they may be natural taste enhancers, such as brewer's yeast, garlic, and animal digests.

Life-Cycle Nutrition

The nutrient contents of commercial cat foods are also formulated to meet specific life-cycle needs of cats, from kittens through old age. This is important because *good nutrition* is a relative term that depends a great deal on a cat's age, activity level, and current state of health. In other words, what's good for a kitten is not necessarily the best choice for an older cat, and vice versa.

In fact, research has shown that certain nutrients consumed at levels that are too high or too low during early life stages may contribute to health problems in later life. This knowledge ended the old womb-to-tomb practice of feeding cats one food their entire lives, and ushered in a new era of life-cycle nutrition.

Today, life-cycle formulas scientifically tailored to meet a cat's nutritional needs during different stages of its life compete for grocery store shelf space. A pet food label states whether the product is formulated for *growth and reproduction, adult maintenance,* or for *all life stages of the cat.* Most manufacturers make product lines geared to all three.

Growth and reproduction formulas are made specifically to satisfy the extra nutrient requirements of growing kittens and breeding or pregnant queens (female cats). Foods formulated for all life stages of cats meet these same requirements, because they must satisfy the range of nutritional needs for cats of all ages. However, adult maintenance formulas are intended primarily for fully grown, nonbreeding, and generally less active felines. This means that foods labeled for adult maintenance do not have to meet the higher nutrient requirements of growth and reproduction formulas. For this reason, adult maintenance diets are *not* satisfactory fare for kittens or pregnant cats.

Feeding Kittens

For their first full year, kittens should receive a high-quality commercial cat food formulated for feline growth. At least 30 to 40 percent of the kittens' diets should be protein to meet the extra demands of their active, rapidly growing bodies. Cat foods guaranteed to be complete and balanced for all life stages of the cat are suitable for kittens, but as previously discussed, adult maintenance formulas are not. Diets for adult cats are generally designed to offer less protein and energy than kittens need to sustain normal, healthy growth.

Calcium and phosphorus are important minerals for strong bones and teeth, normal blood clotting, and proper nerve transmission. A deficiency during a kitten's first year can produce soft, deformed bones. To avoid irreversible skeletal abnormalities, kittens need, for their first full year, a high-quality, commercial cat food designed specifically to support feline growth. So, when selecting a food for your kitten, make sure the product is labeled either for *growth and reproduction* or for *all life stages of the cat.*

Aside from being made to meet the specific nutrient and energy requirements of growing kittens, dry kitten kibble is also patterned into smaller pellets that makes it easier for tiny kitten mouths to chew and swallow. For the first several weeks of life, mother's milk supplies all the nutrients and calories growing kittens need. The queen will suckle them for six or seven weeks, but usually by four weeks of age, kittens can begin experimenting with small amounts of soft, solid foods. To

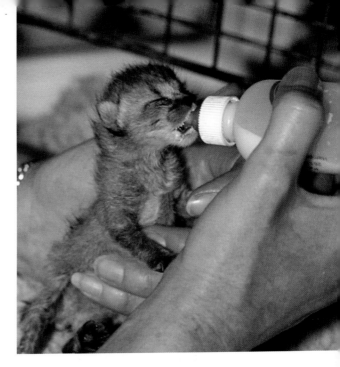

avoid upsetting the kittens' digestive systems, the change to solid food is made gradually over a one- or two-week period.

How much to feed kittens: Because they have smaller stomachs, kittens need to be fed in smaller quantities than adult cats, but their higher energy demands require more frequent feedings to sustain normal growth. Newly weaned kittens will need three or four small meals a day, or leave out dry food for them to eat free-choice. At six months, reduce the number of feedings to two a day. By this age, kittens are almost fully grown but are still quite active and playful. Because their energy demands remain high, continue feeding an appropriate kitten food for another six months. To

determine the proper amount to feed, follow the general feeding recommendations on the pet food package, but be prepared to adjust the amount, as necessary, to meet each individual kitten's needs. During their vital growth and development stage, it's a good idea to offer kittens as much food as they want to eat. Unlike puppies, kittens are not gorge feeders and usually do a good job of self-regulating the amount they eat according to how much energy they burn.

Feeding Pregnant Cats

During periods of gestation (pregnancy) and lactation (nursing), breeding females (called queens) ideally should receive a high-quality food formulated for feline growth and reproduction. Foods labeled *for all life stages of the cat* must meet the same requirements as growth and reproduction formulas; therefore, these products are also sufficient. Because of the extra demand placed on their bodies, pregnant and nursing cats need more calories and high-quality protein to aid in fetal development and milk production. Again, follow the feeding guidelines on the package, adjusting the portions as needed. As with growing kittens, you should allow pregnant cats free access to as much food as they want to eat.

Some breeders believe that queens need calcium supplements during lactation to prevent a condition called eclampsia, or milk fever. This potentially fatal condition occurs when the queen's system is depleted of the essential nutrient, calcium. However, unless advised by a veterinarian, regular supplementation is usually neither necessary nor recommended when feeding a complete and balanced cat food formulated specifically for reproduction. Diets formulated for this particular life stage contain enough calcium to meet the extra needs during pregnancy and lactation.

Feeding Moderately Active Cats

Adult, nonbreeding cats need enough nutrients, fiber, and protein to satisfy their appetites, yet prevent them from getting fat. While a food formulated for all life stages of cats may be fine for many adult felines—especially for the very active breeds—some cats tend to become overweight, particularly during middle age. For cats that tend to be laid-back as individuals and moderately active in their adult years, a suitable commercial food formulated for adult maintenance may be an appropriate choice, especially if the cat starts gaining too much weight.

Adult maintenance formulas are generally adequate for a sedentary, nonbreeding adult cat's lower energy and calorie requirements, and because these diets have fewer calories, they are often a good choice for cats with a weight problem, but before switching diets, first discuss the issue with your veterinarian. Your veterinarian can best assess your cat's weight, body con-

dition, and nutritional needs at any given age and recommend an appropriate feeding regimen.

Remember, adult maintenance formulas are never suitable for growing kittens or pregnant cats because they contain less protein than either the growth and reproduction foods or foods that are formulated for all life stages.

Feeding Older Cats

Cats are generally considered middle-aged at about six or seven years, and seniors at about age ten, although this can vary with the individual. The average life expectancy of the cat is ten to fifteen years, but with today's better nutrition and veterinary care, it's not uncommon for some cats to live twenty years or longer.

As with people, a cat's rate of metabolism gradually slows with age, and the activity level declines as well. The organs typically become less efficient at digesting food or clearing waste products from the body. These physical changes may require some important adjustments to the cat's daily diet to ensure continued good health.

Maintaining weight: Foods labeled *for all life stages* are designed to meet the needs of cats of all ages, from kittens through senior adulthood. But cats, like people, age differently, so there is no single pet food or special senior formula that is suitable for all older cats. Because energy needs decline with less activity, some middle-aged

middle age than they are at an advanced age. Research has shown that digestibility, or the ability to efficiently extract and utilize nutrients in food, tends to decline with age. Many older cats have to eat more to get enough energy, because they don't digest their food as well as they used to. This explains why some elderly cats begin to lose weight and get thin in their later years, after age 11 or so, even though they check out as basically healthy with no dental problems, diabetes, kidney disease, or other health conditions. Because their organs can no longer handle food as efficiently as when they were younger, they simply cannot get the same nutrient value from the same food.

If your senior cat starts to grow thin, but otherwise checks out healthy at the veterinarian's office and has no signs of kidney disease or other medical problems, you definitely don't want to continue feeding a senior or adult maintenance formula that contains fewer calories. Instead, consider switching to an energy-dense food formulated to provide optimum digestibility. Ask your veterinarian to recommend a suitable brand. Often, a good-quality kitten food or feline growth and reproduction formula may do the job. This recommendation contradicts what some owners may have heard or read about always selecting lower-protein foods to ease the burden on an older cat's kidneys. To clarify this misconception, there is no definitive proof that the higher pro-

and senior cats may require fewer calories to avoid becoming obese. For older cats that tend to get fat, an adult maintenance food may be as good a choice as any, or they may thrive on a high-fiber, reduced-calorie light or senior specialty formula. The higher fiber content in some of these diets is designed to satisfy the cat's appetite so that the animal doesn't feel hungry, even though he is consuming fewer calories, less fat, and generally a little less protein. Veterinarians dispense therapeutic diets specially designed to manage a variety of health conditions common in older cats, including weight problems, so at each annual veterinary checkup, be sure to ask if your middle-aged or older cat needs a change in diet.

Losing weight: Not all cats have a weight problem when they get older. In fact, more cats are fat at tein content of certain foods causes renal problems. It is true, however, that once a cat has exhibited signs of renal dysfunction, he definitely requires a lower-protein therapeutic diet to manage the condition and to avoid further compromising the kidneys' ability to process body waste products. Certain other medical conditions may require special diets as well. Your veterinarian can best evaluate your cat's needs in this regard.

If an older cat is otherwise healthy, a higher-protein food, such as one formulated for kittens or for all life stages, is not necessarily detrimental. The point, however, is that before switching to a richer, energy-dense food, it's a good idea to have the cat checked by a veterinarian first to determine his health status and to rule out any underlying health problems. Sometimes, kidney problems don't even become readily apparent until well over half of the normal renal function is lost. Symptoms of kidney dysfunction include increased thirst, increased urination, weight loss, and intermittent vomiting.

Loss of appetite: As with cats of all ages, a sudden loss of appetite in the elderly cat may be a sign that the animal is sick or in pain. Often, an older cat may refuse to eat if he has developed dental disease. Sore gums and aching teeth may simply make eating too painful. Even more serious is the possibility that bacteria from inflamed gums (gingivitis) may leak into the bloodstream and damage other organs. To avoid such problems, have your cat's condition

assessed regularly by a veterinarian, who is the best judge of your cat's overall condition and dietary needs.

Making Dietary Changes

With so many life-cycle choices, product lines, flavors, and varieties to choose from, the important thing to remember is that no one perfect pet food exists for every cat and for every owner. That's why it is necessary for you to ask your veterinarian to reevaluate your cat's condition

from time to time, as your cat's nutritional needs vary, and recommend any appropriate dietary changes.

Make recommended changes to your cat's diet gradually, over a period of at least a week or more. Sudden changes in diet or feeding routine may result in symptoms of gastrointestinal upset in some animals, or your cat may simply refuse to eat the new food. So begin making any dietary change by mixing small amounts of the new food with your cat's current rations. Gradually, over a period of a week or two, increase the amount of new food as you decrease the amount of old food until the changeover is complete.

Deciphering a Cat Food Label

Now that you know about life-cycle feeding and about the nutrients cats need, how can you tell by reading a label whether you've picked a pet food that's right for your cat? Pet food companies are required by law to supply certain nutritional information on their labels, such as the life-stage disclosures that we've already discussed.

The meaning of *complete and balanced:* A pet food label must also disclose whether the food is formulated to provide *complete and balanced* nutrition. The word *complete* means the food has all the necessary nutrients a cat needs for good health. The word *balanced*

means those necessary nutrients are present in the proper proportions. Look for these words on any cat food you buy. If the label doesn't say the food is complete and balanced, chances are, it isn't. Foods that are not complete and balanced may be satisfactory as treats, but they should not be fed as daily rations.

Statement of nutritional adequacy: To prove that their products comply with nutritional guidelines set forth by AAFCO, and to substantiate claims of *100% complete and balanced nutrition,* pet food manufacturers must either adhere to a proven formula or subject their products to lengthy feeding trials with live animals. Of the two, feeding trials offer more assurance that the food is adequately nutritious, because the product has been test-fed to cats for a period of time under AAFCO protocols. Any product that has undergone feeding trials says so on the package. Look for the company's statement of nutritional adequacy, which should say something similar to: *Animal feeding tests using AAFCO procedures substantiate that [this brand name] provides complete and balanced nutrition for the maintenance of adult cats.*

Guaranteed analysis: The required guaranteed analysis must state on the label only whether minimum or maximum amounts of nutrients, in percentages, were met. It doesn't have to list actual concentrations of specific nutrients. The problem with not knowing how much a product exceeds the mini-

mum requirement for a certain nutrient, such as protein, is that sometimes too much can be just as bad as too little, depending on the cat's age and condition. What that means is that, while foods formulated for *all life stages of cats* are designed to meet normal nutritional needs of cats of all ages, some individuals, particularly older ones or those predisposed to certain health problems, may get far more of certain nutrients than they need.

Ingredients list: Ingredients are supposed to be listed in descending order of predominance by weight; however, this can be somewhat misleading. For example, meat may be listed first, leading the consumer to believe the product contains mostly meat, when in reality, the summation of separately listed grains and cereals makes plant material the predominant ingredient. Some labeling terms are strictly regulated; others are not. For example, the title wording of *Chicken for Cats, Chicken Platter, Chicken Entree,* and so forth, can have different meanings in terms of the percentage of chicken the product must contain. A good way to check specific ingredient amounts is simply to call the manufacturer's toll-free number listed on the package and ask for the data. Many companies have consulting veterinarians or nutritionists, and you can judge for yourself how willing and able they seem to be in sharing information and answering your questions. A manufacturer's long-standing reputation can offer some assurance that correct product standards are met and maintained.

Dry weight analysis: Because label percentages are based on the entire food formula, water and all, one must standardize the base of comparison when reading labels of dry, canned, and semimoist foods, in order to analyze and compare the ingredients. This is done by calculating the dry weight, the food content that would be left if all of the water were removed. First, determine the percentages of moisture and dry matter in the food. The guaranteed analysis already contains part of this information. If the label says the moisture content is 78 percent, subtract that figure from 100 percent (total food formula) to calculate the dry matter. In this case, the dry matter in the food is 22 percent.

Once you've calculated the dry matter, you can do a dry weight analysis for each nutrient in the food, based on the label guarantees. The formula for this is simple:

$$\frac{\% \text{ Nutrient}}{\% \text{ Dry Matter}}$$ or the nutrient percentage divided by the dry matter percentage

For example, we've already determined that the dry matter is 22 percent; now we want to know how much of that matter is protein. The guaranteed analysis on the label says the food contains a minimum of 10 percent crude protein. (The word *crude* simply means the maximum or minimum amount was determined by laboratory assay.) That 10 per-

cent figure is based on the food's total formula, including moisture content. However, on a dry matter basis, the protein content is:

$$\frac{10\% \text{ protein}}{22\% \text{ dry matter}}$$ or **.10** divided by **.22** equals **.45** or 45%

To support normal growth and reproduction, AAFCO recommends that at least 30 percent of a cat's diet be protein. For maintenance of adult cats, protein content should be at least 26 percent. These are recommended minimum amounts, based on dry matter, foods should contain. In the above example, the label guarantees the product to be no less than 45 percent protein (dry weight basis), but it doesn't tell you whether the actual protein content exceeds that percentage. This information might be important if, for example, your cat requires a protein-reduced diet.

Dry weight analysis is a good way to compare nutrient percentages in different types of foods, but it's not an exact measurement of daily nutrient intake. Remember, label guarantees are expressed either in minimum (not less than) or maximum (not more than) percentages, but not in actual amounts. If you're concerned about feeding too much or too little of a certain ingredient, consult your veterinarian, who can best judge your cat's individual nutritional needs.

Although pet food labels provide helpful information, choosing a cat food solely by label contents or

Generally speaking, a cat is at his optimum weight when you cannot see the ribs, but can feel them without probing through thick layers of fat (see page 95). Here again, your veterinarian can best judge your cat's overall body condition, so be sure to ask about your cat's weight and discuss your feeding regimen at each annual veterinary checkup.

brand name is unwise. Instead, always base your selection on how well your cat performs and maintains its overall condition on a particular food. Start with a high-quality kitten food that your veterinarian recommends. Then, during annual checkups, as your veterinarian assesses your cat's condition, remember to ask about your cat's changing dietary needs as he reaches adulthood and matures into middle and old age.

Feeding Guidelines

As a guide to daily rations, follow the feeding instructions on the pet food package and measure out the recommended portions. Keep in mind that product-feeding guidelines are based on average nutritional needs and, therefore, are not intended to be used as absolute amounts. Some individuals may need greater portions, some less. Because the amount of food your cat requires each day will vary with its age, weight, and activity level, you may need to adjust the rations to maintain optimum body weight and condition. By starting with the feeding guidelines and adjusting the amount fed as needed, based on how well your cat maintains his body condition, you are less likely to underfeed or overfeed.

As previously discussed, young kittens need frequent small meals, but most adult cats thrive on two meals a day, morning and evening. Other cats do well on a canned food breakfast, combined with ample dry food left out for free-choice nibbling.

Whatever routine works best for you and your cat, your cat will feel more secure if you feed him at the same time and in the same place each day.

Are Homemade Diets Okay?

Because food is often viewed as a symbolic love offering, many people like to express their affection for their cats by preparing home-cooked meals and snacks for them, but constructing a complete and balanced meal for a cat from scratch is not as easy as it sounds. It is a chore best left to the experts. Being carnivores, cats cannot adapt safely to a vegetarian diet, nor can they thrive solely on people food. Their nutritional needs are significantly dif-

ferent from those of humans, dogs, and other mammals.

Without expert guidance, the home-based chef cannot guarantee a complete and balanced mix of proteins, carbohydrates, fats, vitamins, minerals, and amino acids. And because the feline diet requires a delicate balance of numerous ingredients to maintain proper body functions and cell growth, too much or too little can be harmful. For this reason, home-cooked diets should be fed only in rare situations, such as when a cat is suspected of being allergic to an ingredient common in commercially prepared foods. Even then, the makeup of any routine homemade feline diet requires close supervision by a veterinarian with some expertise in animal nutrition.

This does not mean, however, that your cat is barred from ever

sampling your home cooking or from tasting any tidbits of people food. On the contrary, such treats are fine on occasion, as long as you don't overdo it. Just keep the portions small, and don't make such offerings a daily habit, or your cat may begin turning up his nose at his own food. Remember, table scraps and people foods do not provide a complete and balanced diet for cats.

Avoiding Finicky Behavior

Offering too much people food too often can also create a finicky eater, if the cat begins to snub his own food and hold out for the tasty stuff from your meals. Well known for their finicky eating habits, cats do have a discriminating sense of taste, although most of them are not really as finicky as advertisements would lead us to believe. However, feline taste preferences, once developed, can be difficult to change. A cat fed the same type or flavor of food all his life may steadfastly refuse any sort of dietary change, even if his health depends on it. To avoid creating finicky eating behaviors, and to provide variety and appetite appeal, select two or three high-quality products your cat seems to like and use them interchangeably. Alternating a few varieties of cat foods and flavors from kittenhood on will go a long way toward preventing your cat from becoming addicted to one type of food.

The Importance of Water

Water, although sometimes the most overlooked and neglected nutrient, is perhaps the most important dietary element of all. It is more essential for survival than food. Animals have been known to subsist for weeks without food, but most cannot last for more than a few days without water. Water is fundamental to the digestion of food. In fact, digestion begins when enzymes secreted in water start dissolving food. This life-giving liquid is also a principal component of blood, transporting vital nutrients to the cells. Without water, the furnace, or nucleus, in the body's cells will not fire properly and perform the complex chemical reactions necessary to process and use nutrients at the cellular level.

Having evolved from desert animals, cats can conserve water efficiently. They can metabolize water from food and concentrate their urine to very high levels. But this ability doesn't mean that they can go more than a few days without drinking water before becoming dehydrated. Cats can also become dehydrated and require medical attention if they lose too much water through their feces during bouts of diarrhea, or if they suffer severe bouts of vomiting.

Because excessive amounts of minerals have been implicated as a cause of feline lower urinary tract disease, some people give their cats mineral-free bottled water as a precaution. While certainly not harmful, this expensive practice is not necessary, unless you happen to live in an area where the drinking water has an abnormally high mineral content, in which case the drinking water would probably not be the most desirable for human consumption either. Here's a good rule to follow: If the water isn't fit for you to drink, don't let your cat drink it.

Amount of water: The amount of water a cat needs varies with its age, health, and activity level. Climatic conditions and the kind of food a cat eats also influence water consumption. Canned cat food generally contains a moisture content of 78 percent or less. Dry and semi-moist foods, of course, contain much less. Regardless of the type of food fed, always provide a plentiful source of clean, fresh water, preferably in a tip-proof bowl. Self-waterers, which dispense water into a bowl from an inverted bottle, are handy for multicat households and for times when you have to be away from home on an overnight trip.

Become familiar with your cat's drinking habits so you can report any noticeable change to your veterinarian. Excessive thirst and the ensuing frequent urination are symptoms of some serious disorders, such as diabetes and kidney failure, which require immediate medical attention.

Milk: Milk is no substitute for water, nor is it a complete and balanced diet for adult cats. Some adult cats, like some people, develop a lactose intolerance to milk and will experience diarrhea if they drink it. Milk is useful as a temporary supplement for newly weaned kittens, but use a canned kitten milk replacer, available through veterinarians or pet stores, or a half-and-half mixture of evaporated milk and warm water (see page 174).

What Not to Feed Your Cat

Dog Food

Dog foods are scientifically formulated for dogs, *not* cats. Dog chow simply does not contain enough protein, taurine, B-complex vitamins, and essential fatty acids to promote good health in cats. Depending on their age, health, and activity level, cats need at least one and one-half to two times more protein than dogs do. Cats also require the amino acid taurine in their diets, which dogs do not.

When cats and dogs live together, a dog often will develop a liking for cat food, simply because the higher protein content of cat food makes it taste better than dog chow. If your dog starts stealing food from your cat, place the cat's dish out of the dog's reach, either in a separate area or higher up, such as on a countertop. Likewise, discourage your cat from sampling too much of the dog's food, and thus spoiling his appetite for a balanced cat food meal. If you

have a dog and a cat, provide each with his own food, and feed them in separate locations if they steal each other's food.

Vitamin and Mineral Supplements

Vitamin and mineral supplements, unless recommended by a veterinarian, are not necessary when you feed your cat a high-quality, nutritionally complete and balanced commercial cat food. To compensate for nutrient losses during processing, pet food manufacturers add vitamins and minerals to their formulas to supplement natural nutrients contained in the primary ingredients. So, if you add more through additional supplementation—unless necessary to treat a specific condition—the balanced proportions of certain nutrients that your cat is receiving in his food could actually become unbalanced.

Oversupplementing: Responsible cat food manufacturers go to a lot of trouble and expense to back claims that their products are nutritionally complete and balanced for the stated life cycle, so for the most part, you can rely on a brand-name manufacturer's long-standing reputation that these claims are not grossly overstated. And generally speaking, dietary excesses pose more of a problem in many cases than do dietary deficiencies. Therefore, when feeding your cat proper amounts of high-quality commercial cat foods, vitamin and mineral supplements are unnecessary, unless prescribed by a veterinarian for treatment of a specific deficiency. In fact, oversupplementing a cat's diet can cause serious health problems, whether you use natural ingredients or over-the-counter drugs. Too much of a good thing can be just as harmful as too little. For example, a diet too lavish in organ meats, particularly liver, a rich source of vitamin A, can cause an excessive buildup of vitamin A, a condition called hypervitaminosis, in the body tissues. Untreated, this condition can result in painful and crippling skeletal changes. Of course, an occasional meal of liver or other organ meats, thoroughly cooked, but never raw, is okay; just don't overdo it.

Calcium and phosphorus: Certain minerals, such as calcium and phosphorus, must work together in balanced proportions to build strong teeth and bones, aid in blood clotting, and maintain proper nerve transmission. Oversupplementing one nutrient or the other can throw this delicate ratio seriously out of kilter and result in impaired metabolic processes. Excessive amounts of either mineral also can inhibit the body's absorption of magnesium and other minerals.

Some people mistakenly assume that kittens need calcium supplements to grow strong bones and

teeth; however, a good-quality commercial kitten food or growth formula cat food contains all the extra protein and minerals a growing kitten needs. The same is true for a pregnant and nursing queen. As long as you're feeding her a high-quality cat food designed for feline reproduction, no supplements should be required, unless your veterinarian specifically recommends it.

Vitamin D: Vitamin D must be present in adequate amounts for effective absorption and utilization of calcium and phosphorus, but an oversupply can create abnormal calcium deposits in the bones and soft tissues. Weakness, joint pain, and stiffness may indicate vitamin D toxicity. Cortisone helps relieve the pain, but once abnormal calcification has occurred, the damage to body tissues and organs is not so easily undone.

To prevent these vitamin toxicities, avoid using cod-liver oil and other fish-liver oils, which are rich sources of vitamin A and D, as daily dietary supplements. Some breeders may still recommend these substances as a way to improve the sheen of a show cat's coat. However, feeding your cat a high-quality cat food will do more for its coat and overall appearance than any arsenal of vitamin and mineral supplements. A cat with a dry, brittle, or lackluster coat should be examined by a veterinarian, who can diagnose and properly treat the specific cause. The cause of a dull coat may have nothing to do with dietary deficiencies, in which case, arbitrary supplementation by the owner would be futile, potentially dangerous, and a waste of money.

Of course, some cats may require supplementation under certain circumstances. For example, the nutritional needs of a show cat may change during show season when he is subjected to the stresses of extensive travel and ring competition. Cats recovering from illness or injury may require temporary supplementation, but always in such cases, supplementation is safest when given under the advice and guidance of a veterinarian.

Raw Meats

Meat alone is not a balanced meal, and if served raw or undercooked, may contain disease-causing organisms, such as salmonella bacteria and the parasite that causes toxoplasmosis (see page 55). Raw organ meats especially tend to harbor roundworm larvae.

Salmonella bacteria can cause a wide range of intestinal disorders ranging from uncomplicated diarrhea to life-threatening systemic illness. Although cats appear to be highly resistant to the bacteria, they can contract infection from eating contaminated raw or undercooked meats, raw eggs, and infected prey animals. Because the bacteria can spread from cat to cat owner, owners must observe a high level of household hygiene whenever a cat show symptoms of illness. Affected cats shed the bacteria in their feces; therefore, litterboxes should be cleaned and disinfected promptly. Again, owners should always wash hands with soap and water after handling an ill cat and after emptying litter box wastes.

Raw Egg Whites

In addition to the risk of salmonella, raw egg whites contain a protein, called avidin, that can interfere with the body's absorption of the vitamin biotin. A water-soluble member of the B-complex, biotin aids in the synthesis of vitamin C and works in conjunction with other nutrients to keep a cat's skin and coat healthy. Signs of biotin deficiency may include dry, scaly skin, thinning fur, discharges around the nose, eyes, and mouth, small skin lesions, bloody diarrhea, and appetite and weight loss. While eggs are a good source of protein and fat for cats, they should be cooked first and never fed raw. In fact, a well-cooked whole egg added to the diet no more than twice a week may even improve coat sheen.

Raw Fish or All-fish Diets

Feeding cats raw fish exclusive of other foods can cause a thiamine (vitamin B1) deficiency. An enzyme, called thiaminase, found in many kinds of raw fish, can destroy thiamine in the body and produce degenerative disease in the brain and central nervous system. Signs of thiamine deficiency include appetite loss, vomiting, seizures, and loss of coordination. An affected

cat often tucks in its head and curls its body into a ball when picked up. Left untreated, the disorder is fatal. Treatment consists of injections of thiamine or vitamin B-complex, but advanced neurologic damage is often irreversible. Fortunately, commercial cat foods contain adequate amounts of thiamine to make this condition extremely rare.

Canned tuna: A daily diet of canned tuna meat meant for human consumption can also cause vitamin E deficiency in cats. Even cat foods rich in red tuna meat should not be fed exclusive of other flavors and varieties, no matter how fond your feline is of the taste. As the body oxidizes the high amount of unsaturated fatty acids found in tuna, fat-soluble vitamin E is destroyed. If the cat continues to receive excessive amounts of these fatty acids on an all-fish diet, steatitis, or yellow fat disease, may result. The resulting vitamin E deficiency becomes apparent first with flaky skin and a greasy, dull hair coat. As the disease progresses, yellow, lumpy fat deposits appear under the skin, producing an inflammatory reaction and inducing a painful response when the cat is stroked. The disease is easily prevented by avoiding an all-fish diet.

Although fish and tuna varieties of commercial cat foods generally contain adequate thiamine, vitamin E, and other supplements to guarantee complete and balanced nutrition, rotating these flavors with others containing beef, chicken, turkey, and so forth, is wise. Remember, no single brand or variety of cat food can meet all nutritional requirements for *all* cats *all* of the time. By offering at least minimal variety, you help ensure that you're covering all nutritional bases for your cat.

Chocolate

Although a favorite treat for humans, chocolate is *definitely* the wrong choice of snack for your cat. Chocolate contains a natural stimulant, called theobromine, that can be, in sufficient amounts, toxic to cats and dogs. Theobromine constricts the blood vessels, diminishing the flow of the vital fluid to the brain and heart. When ingested, the substance has been known to cause heart attacks in animals. Experts say that theobromine is more concentrated in baking chocolate squares than in regular candies and desserts, where sugar and other ingredients make up more of the recipe. Even small amounts of chocolate can cause vomiting and gastrointestinal upset when consumed by the cat that discovers a chocolate-frosted cake left uncovered on the kitchen counter. So why give your cat an opportunity to develop a liking for something potentially harmful in the first place? Keep candies, baking chocolate, frosted cakes, and other chocolate-flavored desserts covered and safely out of reach.

Alcohol

Alcohol is toxic to cats, even in small amounts, so never allow your party guests to offer your cat a little lap of spiked eggnog, beer, or martini. A cat's slight body mass cannot adequately absorb the intoxicating ingredients in alcohol, and he may quickly become tipsy and develop life-threatening breathing problems. While some ill-informed people may find it amusing to watch a cat stagger in drunken circles, this practice is cruel, dangerous, and sometimes deadly. It takes only a "little hair of the dog" to affect a small animal's breathing, cause shock, and lead to death.

Tobacco and Other Drugs

Keep ashtrays emptied of cigarette butts so that your cat won't be tempted to eat or play with them. Tobacco can be quite toxic to cats, causing drooling, shaking, twitching,

and staggering. To counteract the effects of nicotine poisoning, a veterinarian must administer specific chemical injections. Also, if you smoke, avoid doing so in the presence of your cat, because second-hand smoke is as unhealthful for your pet as it is for humans.

As one might expect, cocaine, marijuana, and similar illegal substances, particularly the inhalant varieties, are potentially dangerous to cats. Furthermore, the deliberate or forced exposure of an animal to such substances can be construed as cruelty to animals, and you could be held legally accountable for such a crime. Signs of marijuana poisoning include behavioral changes, tremors, and convulsions. Specific medical antidotes and supportive care must be given to counteract the plant's toxins.

Bones and Garbage

Garbage is garbage, so don't feed your cat spoiled food or table scraps that you would not eat. Despite the fact that cats in the wild consume the bones of their live prey, never offer your cat any bones left over from your own meals. Chicken and turkey bones in particular are large and brittle enough to splinter and lodge in your cat's throat or puncture parts of the digestive tract. Keep tight lids on all trash containers (inside and outside) so that your cat and other foraging animals will not accidentally consume inedible substances that could cause illness or even death.

Chapter Five

Keeping Your Cat Fit

Fat Cats

Obesity, the accumulation of too much body fat, is considered the number one nutritional disorder among pets today in the United States. As in people, the extra poundage puts pets at higher risk for certain health conditions, such as diabetes, heart disease, lameness, and joint problems, among other ills. Experts also warn that obesity can increase the risk of anesthesia and surgical complications. Because of the added health risks, being overweight may even contribute to a shorter lifespan in cats, just as it can for people. That's why it's so important to be able to recognize when your cat is overweight, and then take corrective action, as recommended by your veterinarian, to remedy the condition.

Assessing Body Condition

How can you tell for sure if your cat is too fat and needs to go on a diet? Numbers alone do not tell the whole story. Normal, fit adult cats, depending on their breed, gender, build, and bone structure, may weigh anywhere from 5 to 40 pounds (2.2 to 18 kg), although the average weight for most cats is probably between 7 and 12 pounds (3.2 to 5.4 kg). Because some breeds are heavier boned than others, they may look stocky and chunky but still be at their ideal weight. Longhaired cats also can appear to be fat when they really aren't, because their fluffy fur makes them look larger. Similarly, the slender Oriental breeds may appear too thin when really they are trim and fit for their breed standard.

The best way to judge whether a cat is overweight or underweight is to visually assess his body condition, but this task is not as easy as it sounds. Studies have shown that a significant number of owners are poor judges of their animal's weight status. They may perceive their cat as well fed and fit when really he is much too tubby. So, if you're unsure whether your cat is at ideal weight, simply ask your veterinarian. A trained practitioner can best assess your cat's overall fitness and body condition.

Signs of Obesity

In general, a cat is too fat if you cannot feel his ribs without having to probe with your fingers through thick, fleshy layers. Fat cats also often have sagging, pendulous bellies, bulges around the neck, and heavy accumulations of fat at the base of the tail. Fit cats, on the other hand, have a discernible waist—a slight dip in their sides just behind the ribs—when viewed from above. While you cannot see the ribs, you can easily feel the ribs with your fingers, as the ribs of a fit cat are padded by only a minimal covering of normal body fat. A cat that is too thin has visible ribs—unless he is longhaired, of course—covered by little or no fat.

Typically, too, fat cats are less active and more lethargic than fit cats. Their cumbersome body mass makes getting around more difficult for them. This decline in exercise and normal activity only exacerbates their overweight problem and contributes to joint stiffness and stress already aggravated by excess weight. Some overweight cats even begin to experience skin and coat problems, because their decreased flexibility makes it too difficult for them to do as good a job of self-grooming. In morbidly obese animals, sores may even appear under folds of fat where the skin cannot properly air out.

Depending on the climate and environment, fat cats may even pant more because their excess body fat makes them less tolerant to heat. Their breathing also may be noticeably more labored, because of the additional stress and pressure placed on their body organs. Because shortness of breath can also be a sign of heart problems caused by fluid buildup in the chest cavity, have a veterinarian examine your cat to rule out serious, underlying medical problems before putting the animal on any kind of weight-reduction program.

Causes of Obesity

Cats get fat for basically the same reasons people do: too much food and too little exercise. However, as in people, the condition can be quite complex, and more factors than just the amount of calories in and calories out can play a role in the development of the obese cat.

Heredity: An individual cat's breed and genetics may predispose him to becoming a fat cat. Some active breeds, such as the Siamese

and the Abyssinian, are far less prone to putting on excess pounds than their more sedate cousins, the Persians, which are well loved and well known for their quiet, passive, laid-back temperaments. However, almost any cat, whether purebred or of mixed heritage, can become a fat cat under the right circumstances.

Lack of exercise: Available exercise opportunities make a big difference, too. Cats that go outdoors certainly expend more energy hunting prey, climbing trees, and prowling their territories. Although some people may view this as justification for letting their cats roam, outdoor cats are clearly more vulnerable to numerous dangers associated with the outside world. Keeping cats indoors clearly improves their chances of enjoying safer, healthier,

and longer lives, but it's important to substitute appropriate and ample play and exercise opportunities for confined cats, particularly for those living in small apartments. Helping indoor cats stay fit and trim is not difficult at all and can even be a satisfying source of pleasure for both owner and pet. The section on Exercising Your Cat, page 103, covers this subject in more detail.

Medical problems: As is true in people, individual metabolism and certain medical conditions that influence the way the body breaks down and uses food can contribute to obesity in cats. Most notably, these include disorders of the endocrine system or glands. Hypothyroidism, caused by an underactive thyroid gland, slows down the body's metabolism, causing an animal to

gain weight and appear sluggish. Diabetes can also cause weight gain, but it is more commonly associated with weight loss. When evaluating cases of obesity, most veterinarians will screen for these and certain other disorders simply to rule them out, before prescribing any weight-loss program. This is one reason why it is important to have your veterinarian examine your cat, if you suspect he has a weight problem.

Overfeeding: By far, the most common cause of obesity in cats is simply the consumption of too many calories over a period of time. Many cats fed dry food free-choice regulate their own consumption and never develop a weight problem, but others will overeat if given unlimited access to too much food. If yours is one of the latter, make sure that you carefully measure out only the recommended daily ration for your cat

to eat at leisure. Follow the product-feeding guidelines as a general guide for the amount of food you should offer your cat each day. However, keep in mind that every cat is different, and his individual metabolic makeup and energy needs ultimately determine how much food and calories he needs each day. Closely observe your cat's body condition and eating habits and make adjustments as needed.

Competitive eating: In multicat households, competitive eating tends to make some cats overeat. The obvious solution in this case is to feed cats in separate areas, and always use separate bowls, one per cat. If necessary, supervise mealtimes to make sure each cat eats from his own bowl and consumes the proper portions.

Too many treats: Some owners simply offer too much food, while others unwittingly contribute to a

Weight Gain

If weight gain becomes a problem, your veterinarian may recommend that you gradually cut back the amount fed or that you consider using an alternative feeding method. For example, it may become necessary to switch from feeding free-choice to serving meals in controlled portions offered at set mealtimes. When using the latter method, remove any remaining food after about 30 minutes, or when your cat stops eating and walks away from his dish.

weight problem by feeding too many high-fat, gourmet snacks between meals. The habit of overfeeding treats commonly arises as a means of expressing affection, often because the owner has learned from his or her own life experiences to associate food with reward and love. While there is nothing wrong with giving your cat an occasional treat, take care to restrict the amount and frequency so that a weight problem does not develop.

Do not offer treats every day. Instead, reserve them for special occasions, or use them sparingly as rewards. In addition, limit the portions to only a few tasty tidbits at a time. Avoid feeding high-fat people foods, such as french fries, cookies, potato chips, and ice cream. These items are just as fattening and unhealthful for cats as they are for humans. If you're going to give treats, stick with the commercial cat treats concocted especially for the feline palate.

Age: Research has shown that cats in their middle years, between the ages of 6 and 11 years, are more likely to be fat than either younger or older cats. Kittens stay trim by expending lots of calories and energy for growth and play. To a lesser extent, young adult cats continue this energy expenditure for several years as they hunt, prowl, play, and reproduce. But for many cats, the middle years bring with them the middle-age spread, and as some cats creep into old age, they tend to grow thinner with time, because their bodies no longer digest and use nutrients as efficiently. The influence of age factors on dietary needs is one reason why you need to periodically reevaluate your cat's nutritional requirements based on its current life cycle (see page 76).

Altering: The notion that spaying the female cat or neutering the male causes them to get fat has been a long-held myth even though, after numerous studies, definitive proof of this remains elusive. While experts can still say with some certainty that spaying and neutering do not *directly* cause cats to get fat, there is evidence that the absence of gonado-tropic (sex) hormones may alter the body's energy or calorie requirements in some individuals. This means that, while not a direct cause of obesity, these surgical procedures can become influential factors in a weight problem when combined with major contributing causes, such as consistent overfeeding. For this reason, responsible owners need to be aware of this potential so they can watch for signs of weight gain following the operations and, if necessary, adjust their cats' caloric intake accordingly. Always consult a veterinarian first before putting a cat on any special diet, including one designed for weight loss.

Too much of a too-rich diet: The type of food fed to a cat also influences weight. Many of the so-called *premium* or *super-premium* cat foods are more appropriately termed energy-dense, meaning that their richer ingredient mix delivers more

calories and energy per serving. Often, they are designed to be highly digestible, which means that the cat can extract more of the food's nutrient value from smaller portions. This can be a plus, as long as you offer the portions recommended on the package label; however, too many owners who switch to premium foods inadvertently end up overfeeding their pets. This is because they often fail to consult the new package's feeding guidelines and continue to offer the same size portions they've become accustomed to pouring in the bowl each day. And because many premium foods are designed to be highly palatable, some cats tend to eat what's offered with great gusto, simply because the food tastes good. This, of course, tempts their delighted owners to indulge them even more, until overeating and overfeeding become a well-established pattern.

Because feeding directions can vary significantly from one product to another, always read the feeding guidelines on the package before offering any new food product to your cat. If your cat starts to gain weight on any food, whether premium or not, check the guidelines to make sure you're feeding the recommended daily amount. If you determine that you're overfeeding, cut back gradually to the recommended portions.

Weight-Loss Formula Cat Foods

Light Food

Historically, the words *light, lean, reduced*, and similar designations have had little regulatory meaning in the pet food industry. Until a few years ago, AAFCO recommendations required a light cat food to deliver at least 15 percent less energy than the company's regular product. The problem with this definition was that it offered no consistency from one manufacturer to another. For example, a light food produced by one manufacturer could contain more calories than a regular food made by a different manufacturer. To remedy this, AAFCO agreed on new regulations in late 1996 intended to standardize dietary claims on pet food labels so that consumers would be better able to compare like products made by different manufacturers.

The standardized regulations now require that cat food products claiming to be *light, lite,* or *low calorie* meet specific calorie maximum amounts based on the weight of the contents—not the volume—and on the percentage of moisture in the product. While products claiming to have fewer calories or reduced calories aren't held to the same calorie counts as lite or low-calorie foods, they do have to state and substantiate the percentage of reduction along with a basis of comparison.

Calorie Content Statements

Although not required on pet food labels that make no calorie-related claims, calorie content statements, when used on a product claiming to be *light*, *lite*, *low calorie*, *fewer calories*, or *reduced calories* must be substantiated according to AAFCO's regulations. The statement has to appear on the label distinctly apart from the guaranteed analysis. The number of calories also must be measured in terms of metabolizable energy (ME) and expressed in kilocalories per kilogram (kcal/kg). Other common units of measurement, such as kilocalories per cup or pound, may be used in addition to the mandatory kcal/kg ME, or the amount of energy actually used or metabolized by the animal, can be substantiated by calculation or by animal feeding trials.

Low-fat Food

Pet foods that bear lean or low-fat claims must meet certain maximum crude fat percentages based on the product's moisture content, according to AAFCO's guidelines. Such products also have to express minimum and maximum crude fat guarantees in the guaranteed analysis section of the product label. Products claiming to contain less fat or reduced fat must state similar guarantees, plus the percentage of reduction along with a basis of comparison. These are all measures intended to help consumers compare different products.

Veterinary-dispensed Weight-loss Diets

Although an obese cat needs fewer calories and fats, he still requires adequate amounts of protein, vitamins, and minerals to maintain good health. The ideal weight-reduction formula is designed to provide enough of these essential nutrients while restricting caloric intake. Calories come primarily from carbohydrates and fats, so the amounts of these ingredients must be carefully controlled. Because of the restricted amounts of certain ingredients, weight-reduction formulas are not appropriate diets for cats of all life stages. The reduced energy value of weight-reduction foods simply cannot meet the extra needs of growing kittens and pregnant or nursing queens, for example. Nor are weight-loss foods necessarily suit-

able as daily rations for nonbreeding adult cats that do not have a weight problem, or for cats that have other medical problems. For these reasons, many pet food manufacturers design their weight-loss products as therapeutic diets to be dispensed through veterinarians. This way, the veterinarian can evaluate the need for the special diet and properly supervise and monitor the cat's weight-loss progress.

Therapeutic weight-loss cat foods are usually formulated to be relatively low in calories and fat, but higher in fiber. Because fiber is poorly digestible, it delivers fewer calories. The increased amount of dietary crude fiber in these formulas may also help promote a feeling of fullness in the cat so that he doesn't feel deprived and hungry while on the weight-loss program. However, the problem with more fiber is that it produces greater stool volume.

Putting a Fat Cat on a Safe Diet

The owner who arbitrarily reduces a cat's rations or suddenly switches the cat to a weight-loss diet without first consulting a veterinarian is asking for trouble. All changes in diet must be made gradually over a period of one or two weeks by adding and mixing increasing amounts of the new food to decreasing portions of the old food until the switch is complete.

Dieting Dangers

Not only must dietary changes be made gradually, but the rate of weight loss for an obese cat must be gradual, too, and carefully supervised by a medical professional. Too-rapid weight loss, or crash diets, can be potentially harmful, resulting in tissue wasting or causing a condition called hepatic lipidosis, also known as fatty liver disease. As the name implies, fatty liver disease develops when too much fat (lipids) builds up in the liver's cells. The disorder is sometimes seen when a cat, particularly a heavyset feline, suddenly stops eating, and, if the restricted intake is allowed to continue, fat begins to accumulate in the liver. Left untreated, the condition can quickly become life threatening, which is why loss of appetite in the cat should *never* be ignored. Treatment consists of getting the cat to eat again as soon as possible, which may be accomplished by forced oral feeding or by intravenous feeding.

Successful Dieting

The key to success in any feline weight-loss program is owner compliance. The owner must first recognize that the cat is overweight and then be willing to follow a veterinarian's instructions to the letter. From the veterinarian's standpoint, modifying the owner's feeding behavior is sometimes as big a part of the program as prescribing and supervising a proper diet. For example, the owner who reinforces the human-animal bond by offering too many rich treats must learn to replace this habit with other reward actions, such as praise, petting, and grooming. Interestingly, studies show a correlation among overweight pets and overweight owners, suggesting that learned associations linking food offerings with affection may be at work, along with other complex psychological factors.

During treatment, the veterinarian may ask the owner to weigh the cat weekly and keep a detailed record of the type and amounts of all food given. This helps to adjust the weight-loss rate as needed. Weighing a cat can be tricky, because most animals refuse to stand or sit on the scales long enough for you to get a good reading. The easiest way to accomplish weighing in at home is to weigh yourself first on a reliable set of bathroom scales. Then, hold the cat in your arms and step on the scales a second time. Subtracting the difference will give you the cat's weight.

Bulk-feeding or free-choice: While the cat is on the weight-loss diet, it is best to cut out *all* treats and table scraps; however, if you insist on offering them, be sure to include them in your weekly log. Avoid offering food in bulk, as in filling a self-feeder or a large bowl full of several meal portions at one time. If your cat already has a problem self-regulating his food intake, bulk-feeding indiscriminate portions will only encourage overeating and make the problem worse. Free-choice feeding of dry rations is okay, if that is the way your cat is used to being fed, but the key is to measure and leave out only the recommended amount per day, if feeding once a day, or per serving, if feeding at multiple meal-time intervals. That way, your cat can nibble at will, but when the last bit of food is gone from the bowl, he will have eaten only the daily ration or a controlled-portion serving, whichever is the case.

If you have more than one cat, free-choice feeding can present some special problems, since cats in the same household tend to swap and share bowls and eat each other's food. To accommodate one on a special diet, it may be necessary, in some cases, to reconsider how you feed all of your cats. You may have to feed the one on the special diet separately and restrict his access to the other cats' food. Otherwise, the dieter will certainly move over to a buddy's bowl to eat more. In addition, if you allow your cat to go outdoors, supervise his activities so that he won't hunt and scavenge for food, or seek out another meal at a nearby neighbor's house.

Exercising Your Cat

As with human weight-loss programs, exercise is also an important factor in successfully slimming down the tubby tabby. Most obese cats lead sedentary lifestyles. This may be due partly to the cat's personality, or it may be a direct result of lim-ited exercise opportunities available in his environment. For example, the apartment-confined cat has little territory to defend and less room to romp. Certainly, this statement is not meant to imply that confining cats indoors is a bad idea. On the contrary, keeping cats indoors is preferable, because they are less likely to be exposed to parasites or disease, injured in cat fights, hit by cars, attacked by dogs, poisoned by spilled chemicals, or harmed by cruel people. However, the owner of an indoor cat needs to devise

ample exercise opportunities by playing with the cat more and by installing carpeted climbing trees.

1. Provide toys. Inexpensive items, such as catnip-filled sacks, Ping-Pong balls, paper grocery bags, golf balls, tennis balls, and a cardboard box with cut-out peep holes, provide good exercise and fun for cats. When selecting cat toys, always consider safety (see page 43).

2. Play with your cat. Interactive play with your cat can be fun for you and healthy for your cat. The time you enjoy together in this way also helps strengthen the human-animal bond. Use one of those fishing-pole-style toys with a feather, pompom, or sparkler lure attached on the end

of a string and spend short periods each day letting your cat stalk and chase the flying lure. Because strings, sparklers, and feathers can be potentially hazardous to cats if chewed and swallowed, always store this type of toy in a closet, safely out of your cat's reach, when you are not present to supervise play. Any toy with string or yarn is especially dangerous if a cat is left unsupervised with it (see page 43).

3. Give your cat a playmate. Another good way to give your cat exercise is to provide him with a live-in playmate. If you can afford double feed and veterinary bills, keeping two cats instead of one helps ensure that a single feline left at home alone all day does not become bored and lonely. Despite their aloof reputations, cats are highly social animals, and most enjoy the companionship of their own kind, as long as they are properly introduced and socialized. After establishing their own household hierarchy, most cat companions will play together, sleep together, and even groom each other.

Taking Your Cat for Walks

Another good way to exercise your indoor cat and allow him to safely experience the outdoors is to take him for walks on a leash. As odd as the idea may seem, many cats, with patience and perseverance, can learn to enjoy walking on a leash. Just don't expect them to heel with precision by your side the way a trained dog does. Some cats take to walking on a leash better than others, and those that do generally prefer to lead the way. Much depends on individual temperament. And, of course, there will always be certain individuals who simply won't tolerate the notion at all. The best you can hope for is that your cat will learn to tolerate the leash well enough to lead you where he wants to go.

Warning: One thing you should *never* do is tie a cat on a long lead and leave him unattended. Without supervision, a tied cat could become entangled and accidentally strangle or hang himself.

To determine whether your cat will adapt to leash walking, start by selecting an adjustable nylon or leather cat harness and a lightweight leash. Most pet supply stores and catalogs market figure-eight harnesses designed specifically to restrain cats so they can't slip free and escape. Never use a choker collar designed for dogs on a cat. Also, avoid dog harnesses, as cats can easily slip out of them and run away from you.

To begin leash training: Accustom the cat to the harness by putting it on when you're home to supervise. Let the cat drag the leash freely behind him, but don't leave the cat unattended while doing this, because he might get entangled or accidentally hang himself. After the cat is well used to wearing the equipment, begin leading him around indoors on the leash. The best way to accomplish this is to use a pull toy for enticement, gently coaxing the cat to follow you on the leash for short distances. Praise the cat lavishly when he goes in the desired direction. Confine your practice sessions indoors until your cat walks comfortably with you on a leash throughout the house. Only then should you venture outside for short walks, making sure to select a quiet, secluded area so that he won't be frightened by unfamiliar sights and sounds. Until your cat adjusts to the outdoors, take along a pet carrier so that, if something frightens the cat and causes him to struggle on the leash, you can pop him into his carrier for safety. The confinement of the carrier will also serve to calm a scared cat and make him feel more secure.

Chapter Six

Keeping Your Cat Healthy

Choosing a Veterinarian

One of the most important decisions you will make as a cat owner is which veterinarian to visit regularly. Try to make this decision *before* you acquire your cat, because you will want to schedule a post-purchase exam right after you bring your new cat home, within the first week, if possible.

Whether you choose someone in general veterinary practice or someone who treats cats exclusively, make sure you are comfortable with the way the veterinarian deals with you and your cat. For example, at your first appointment, decide whether you feel at ease with the way the doctor addresses your concerns and explains terms, procedures, or findings. Also, note whether the doctor seems willing to take time to answer your questions and share information.

If you're a first-time cat owner, use the visit as an opportunity to ask for advice on cat care and nutrition.

Many veterinarians view pet owner education as an important part of their profession and will hand out brochures and wellness information kits to new clients. Some will recommend good cat care books to read. Others will show videos on everything from diet to dental care. It's important to express your willingness to learn and to establish a good rapport with your veterinarian and his or her staff. Their professional guidance will be a valuable and reliable asset to you as a cat owner.

Ask whether the veterinary clinic offers 24-hour emergency services, and keep the emergency number handy, in case your cat becomes ill or injured. Also, find out whether the clinic offers additional services, such as grooming and boarding, that you might want to use later.

Signs of Illness in the Cat

With proper nutrition, regular veterinary checkups, good dental care, and routine vaccinations, you can reasonably expect your cat to live about 10 to 15 years. While this is average, it is not uncommon for many cats these days to live into their twenties. When illness does strike, however, you must be prepared to recognize the signs and symptoms and seek veterinary care right away. By recognizing a problem readily and seeking treatment early, you can greatly improve your cat's chances for a full recovery.

Changes in appetite: Often, the first telltale sign that something is wrong with your cat is a sudden change in appetite, which is why any marked change in normal eating habits should be regarded with suspicion and carefully watched. If the problem doesn't resolve itself quickly, within 24 hours or so, report your observations to a veterinarian.

Changes in litter box habits: Likewise, sudden changes in toilet habits should be investigated for medical causes. If you notice that your cat is missing the litter box, straining to urinate, urinating more often, passing bloody urine, or urinating in unusual places, suspect a lower urinary tract infection or blockage and seek medical attention right away (see page 118). In aging cats, chronic kidney disease is a common medical problem, and increased urination and weight loss are among the most notable signs.

Other Trouble Signs

In addition to any changes in appetite or litter box habits, other

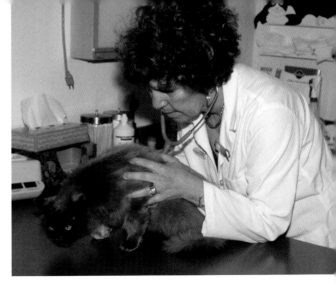

signs and symptoms of illness in the cat include:

- unexplained or rapid weight loss
- increased thirst
- frequent vomiting
- diarrhea
- coughing
- sneezing
- bleeding
- staggering
- swellings
- panting
- lethargy
- lameness
- coat changes
- nasal discharge
- bloody stool
- crouching in a hunched-up position
- hiding in unusual places
- difficulty breathing

The list is by no means complete. Because cats can succumb rapidly to illness, don't delay in seeking veterinary help at the first hint of trouble.

While it's wise to always keep your cat safely indoors, you should especially do so if you suspect an illness, so you can observe him closely. Sick cats often seek seclusion in out-of-the-way places, and if you allow your cat to wander off, you may not find him again until the illness is too advanced to be treated effectively.

Preventive Health Care

You can do three things to help prevent illness and maximize your cat's chances of living a long and healthy life:

1. Get annual veterinary checkups for your cat.

2. Adhere to the routine vaccination schedule your veterinarian recommends.

3. Keep your cat indoors.

These three simple strategies benefit both your cat and your pocketbook. How? First, with regular preventive health care, your cat will have a better shot at living out his full life span. Second, by preventing health problems instead of treating them, you stand to save yourself money in the long run. You don't have to be a mathematician to figure out that the cost of aggressively treating a single serious illness can quickly surpass the money you spend on yearly physicals and routine booster shots throughout your cat's lifetime.

Common sense dictates that an indoor cat is less likely to contract an illness from a free-roaming animal or fall victim to other outdoor hazards. Remember, however, that keeping your cat indoors doesn't mean you can skip routine vaccinations altogether. They are just as important for the indoor cat as the outdoor cat, as the following section explains.

Vaccinations

Several infectious diseases common in cats are caused by airborne organisms that can waft into your home on a breeze through open doors and windows. Even your hands, shoes, and clothing can serve as transmission modes, silently tracking in deadly disease-causing organisms. Fortunately, highly effective vaccines exist to combat many feline diseases, and that's why it's important to keep vaccinations current, based on the booster schedule your veterinarian recommends.

How vaccines work: Vaccines artificially induce active immunity by stimulating the production of antibodies against a specific disease-causing organism. As long as the antibody level remains high enough in the body, the antibodies can attack and overcome a disease organism that attempts to invade. But because this protection wanes over time, your cat needs periodic booster shots throughout his lifetime to maintain an adequate level of antibodies in the system. Your veterinarian will recommend an appropriate vaccination schedule for your cat's individual health care needs.

Passive immunity: A vaccination schedule begins when your cat is a "toddler." Newborn kittens are born with what is called passive immunity, which they acquire from maternal antibodies in their mother's first milk, the colostrum. How long this naturally acquired passive immunity lasts depends upon the antibody level in the mother's blood when the kittens are born. Usually, this protection lasts from 12 to 16 weeks, but it may wear off as early as 8 weeks.

Because kittens are highly susceptible to certain infectious diseases, initial vaccination at around six to eight weeks of age is often recommended to ensure that youngsters remain protected. However, if maternal antibodies are still present in the kitten's system when he receives his first shots, those passive antibodies may render the vaccines ineffective. That's why vaccinations for the common feline res-

piratory infections and feline distemper are repeated until about 12 to 16 weeks of age, to ensure that they take, as well as to provide the kitten with continuous immunity as maternal antibodies wear off.

Establishing initial immunity: The American Association of Feline Practitioners and Academy of Feline Medicine Advisory Panel on Feline Vaccines update feline vaccination guidelines from time to time, as ongoing research reveals new insights and as new or improved vaccines become available. So it's important to check with your veterinarian for the most current information and follow the immunization program that he or she recommends for your cat.

Generally speaking, most experts recommend that kittens under 12 weeks of age (but at least 6 weeks old) begin receiving their primary series of vaccinations for what's called the "core" vaccines—the ones highly recommended for most cats. Typically, the doses are repeated every 3 to 4 weeks until the kitten reaches 12 to 16 weeks old. If the kitten is already older than 16 weeks, two initial doses 3 to 4 weeks apart may be recommended, depending on the vaccine. One year after the last dose of the initial vaccination series, the cat usually needs to receive booster shots, and then after that, no more frequently than every three years, unless recommended otherwise by your veterinarian.

Here, it is worth noting that certain vaccines may require a different dosing schedule for initial immunization or more frequent follow-up booster shots because of the way they are manufactured, which is why you should adhere to your veterinarian's advice on the matter. For example, initial vaccination for rabies (a "core" vaccine because the disease is dangerous and transmissible to humans) depends on the label of the product used, but generally requires two doses 12 months apart. Also, in some regions, the law may require an annual booster for rabies versus one every three years.

Core and noncore vaccines: The so-called "core" vaccines protect against severe or easily transmitted diseases and are highly recommended for most, if not all, cats. The core diseases include rabies, feline panleukopenia virus (also called feline distemper), feline viral rhinotracheitis (also called feline herpesvirus-1), and feline calicivirus. Some of the core vaccines may be combined into one convenient injection, to spare your cat the discomfort of multiple needle pricks. Some vaccines are also available in intranasal form, given as nose drops.

Noncore or ancillary vaccines are considered optional. They may be recommended for cats at highest risk of exposure to certain diseases, such as feline leukemia virus (FeLV), feline immunodeficiency virus (FIV), chlamydia (also known as feline pneumonitis), feline infectious peritonitis (FIP), bordetella bronchiseptica (a respiratory disease), giardia, and ringworm. For example, a cat kept indoors has less chance of exposure to FeLV (and other diseases) than a cat that is allowed to roam freely outside. Any cat that goes outdoors, is frequently boarded, is used for breeding, has contact with other cats (especially free-roaming strays), or lives with a FeLV-positive cat has a greater chance of contracting the disease and would likely benefit from vaccine protection.

An ongoing vaccination schedule: Any change in your cat's lifestyle, such as the addition of a new cat to the family, may require some changes in your ongoing vaccination program, so, at your cat's annual checkup, tell your veterinarian how often your cat goes outdoors, even for short, supervised jaunts; how frequently your cat travels with you; whether you exhibit your pet in cat shows; and how often your pet is exposed to other cats. By knowing these details, your veterinarian can more accurately assess your cat's individual health risks and recommend an appropriate vaccination and booster schedule.

Vaccine reactions: Although side effects from vaccines are minimal in most cases, some cats do seem to be more sensitive to certain vaccines than others, particularly the ones for FeLV and rabies. Regardless of breed, it is fairly common for some cats to experience mild lethargy for a day or two after receiving their shots. But some vaccine reactions can be serious, causing convulsions, labored breathing, and even death. Serious vaccine reactions constitute a true medical emergency, requiring immediate veterinary treatment.

If your cat ever experiences a vaccine reaction, your veterinarian may recommend administering the boosters separately and spacing them apart the next time, so be sure to report any adverse reaction, no matter how mild. To help ensure your cat's safety and comfort, your veterinarian also may premedicate your cat to minimize the severity of any reaction.

Fibrosarcomas: The first FeLV vaccine took about 20 years to develop. Initial immunity is usually established with two injections spaced about a month apart, then maintained by regular boosters.

Although vaccination is considered a highly effective weapon against this devastating illness, recent research has raised concerns about a low incidence of tumors, called fibrosarcomas, developing at the injection sites of FeLV (and rabies) vaccines. While not caused by the vaccines directly, the tumors appear to result from a profound localized inflammation some cats experience, perhaps in reaction to the aluminum compounds used in the vaccine suspension.

As the matter remains under investigation, not all veterinarians recommend FeLV vaccination for *all* cats. Some recommend it only for cats at greatest risk of contracting the disease, which is why the vaccine is considered noncore, or optional. Also, veterinarians avoid

Quick Reference Chart

Feline Diseases	Symptoms	Prognosis
Feline Viral Rhinotracheitis (FVR) (also called Feline herpesvirus): Highly contagious respiratory ailment caused by herpesvirus; core vaccine is preventive	Sneezing, nasal discharge, crusty, watering eyes, appetite loss, lethargy	High mortality rate; survivors may become chronic carriers and shed virus during stress
Feline Calicivirus (FCV): Serious upper respiratory infection; core vaccine is preventive	Similar to FVR, with painful tongue, mouth ulcers, sore muscles, stiff gait, limping	May progress to pneumonia; survivors may become carriers
Feline Panleukopenia Virus (FPV): Also called feline distemper, feline parvovirus (unrelated to canine parvovirus), or feline infectious enteritis; core vaccine is preventive	Appetite loss, fever, depression, vomiting yellow bile, painful abdomen, low white cell count (leukopenia)	Often fatal; highly contagious among cats
Feline Chlamydiosis: Respiratory infection, also called feline pneumonitis; noncore vaccine	Similar to FVR and FCV with weepy eyes, swollen eyelids	Quite contagious, especially among kittens
Rabies: Core vaccine is preventive and required by law in many localities	Personality changes, irritability, paralysis to facial, throat muscles, thick, stringy saliva	Fatal; transmissible to humans and other mammals from infected animal's saliva via bite, open wound, or scrape
Feline Leukemia Virus (FeLV): Noncore vaccine is preventive; testing recommended to determine positive or negative status	Weight loss, anemia, poor appetite, lethargy, recurring infections	Often fatal, but infected cats may survive several years
Feline Infectious Peritonitis (FIP): If exposure risk is high, noncore nose drop vaccine recommended	Fever, lethargy, appetite and weight loss, labored breathing, swollen belly	Potentially fatal; may affect internal organs; poses greatest hazard in multicat households
Feline Immunodeficiency Virus (FIV): Also called feline AIDS, *cannot* be transmitted to humans; keeping cats indoors is preventive	Lethargy, weight loss, gum disease, chronic infections, weakened immune system	No current cure or vaccine; testing recommended to determine status; virus spreads among cats through bites

Feline Diseases	Symptoms	Prognosis
Feline Lower Urinary Tract Disease (FLUTD): Also called feline urologic syndrome or FUS; caused by mineral crystals forming in the urethra	Frequent urination, straining to urinate, passing blood in urine, urinating in unusual places	May lead to urinary blockage, kidney damage, and death if left untreated
Feline Bordetella: Highly infectious upper respiratory disease in cats caused by bacteria, similar to "kennel cough" in dogs. An optional, noncore vaccine is available.	Coughing, sneezing, nasal discharge, fever, loss of appetite	Treatable with antibiotics and nutrition support. Often mild in adults, but can rapidly progress to pneumonia and death in kittens

giving the FeLV vaccine between the shoulder blades because the tumors are less operable there. As part of an effort to standardize vaccine sites, and thus help track adverse reactions, the FeLV injection is now generally given in the cat's left rear leg, while the rabies vaccination is given in the right rear leg.

In deciding whether to vaccinate your cat for the leukemia virus, keep in mind that FeLV is high on the list among the leading causes of death in cats. If your cat gets the disease, there is no cure. When discussing the preferred course of preventive care with your veterinarian, remember also that, according to the experts, the overall incidence of tumor development at the injection site is considered quite low, compared to the number of vaccines given. Unvaccinated cats face a far greater risk of developing fatal diseases if exposed to the virus.

Feline Diseases

Feline Viral Rhinotracheitis (FVR)

Also called feline herpesvirus-1 or simply "rhino," this serious upper respiratory infection caused by a herpes virus is often mistaken by the misinformed for a common cold because symptoms include sneezing, nasal discharge, and crusty, watering eyes. Often, the cat stops eating. Cats don't catch colds as people do, but they can contract viruses, such as rhino, that produce coldlike symptoms; therefore, when such symptoms occur in the cat, immediate medical attention is a must.

Highly contagious, rhino or FVR spreads easily from cat to cat through direct contact with body secretions and contaminated objects, such as litter boxes, feeding bowls, or even human hands. Some cats show only mild symptoms and

recover quickly, while others become progressively worse and may develop severe complications, such as eye ulcers. In some cases, the virus damages the throat, sinus, and nasal structures, leaving the cat prone to repeated bacterial infections in those areas.

Rhino has a high mortality rate among kittens and older cats. Cats that survive the acute illness may become chronic carriers and, during stressful periods, will shed the herpes virus, making them a potential hazard to other cats in the household. The vaccine for this herpes virus is one of the core vaccines, and by far the most effective way to reduce the occurrence and severity of upper respiratory infections is simply to vaccinate all cats.

Feline Calicivirus (FCV)

Like FVR, FCV is a serious upper-respiratory infection with similar symptoms, except FCV is more likely to progress to pneumonia. Painful tongue and mouth ulcers can make the disease particularly disabling, as the cat may refuse to eat or drink. Muscle soreness, exhibited by a stiff gait or limping, also may be present. As with FVR, some cats that recover from the calicivirus may become carriers. The best prevention is administering a core vaccine.

Feline Panleukopenia Virus (FPV)

Perhaps more commonly known as feline distemper or feline parvovirus, FPV bears no relation to the virus that causes distemper in dogs. The disease is destructive, highly contagious, and often fatal. Fortunately, it is less common than it once was, thanks, no doubt, to effective vaccines, which should be a core part of every cat's immunization program.

Without early detection and treatment, the infected cat becomes desperately ill. Onset occurs four to six days after exposure, and early signs may include appetite loss, depression, fever, and vomiting yellow bile. Because the virus often attacks the lining of the small intestine, the disease also is sometimes referred to as feline infectious enteritis. An afflicted cat will show signs of having a painful abdomen and may cry out pitifully if touched in that area. Sick cats have reportedly been observed crouching in a stiff, hunched-up manner over a water bowl, as if wanting to drink but unable to. A lowered white blood cell count (leukopenia) confirms the diagnosis and gives the disease its clinical name.

Feline Chlamydiosis

Sometimes referred to as feline pneumonitis, this respiratory infection is caused by an organism called *Chlamydia psittaci*. With respiratory symptoms similar to those in FVR and FCV, chlamydia infection often begins with weepy eyes and swollen eyelids. The disease can be quite contagious, especially among kittens; however, recent studies indicate that only a small percentage of feline respiratory infections in the United States are actually caused by chlamydia. For this reason, the vaccine is considered noncore, to be optionally administered, based on risk of exposure. As with the other types of respiratory illnesses, the best defense is routine vaccination, which can help lessen the severity of the disease, should it occur.

Rabies

One of the few feline ailments transmissible to humans, rabies occurs in nearly all warm-blooded animals. Skunks, foxes, raccoons, cats, and dogs account for most sporadic outbreaks in the United States. The deadly virus passes from an infected animal's saliva through a bite, open wound, or scrape. People bitten or scratched by a rabid animal must immediately undergo a series of injections in order to save their lives, for beyond a certain stage, the disease is inevitably fatal. Whenever a human life is at stake, an animal suspected of having rabies is humanely destroyed, and its brain tissue is tested to confirm the presence of the virus.

Once inside the body, the virus travels to the brain, where it produces two characteristic forms: furious and paralytic, or dumb, rabies. In the furious phase, cats exhibit personality changes that progress from subtle to severe. While symptoms can vary, normally affectionate and sociable cats may withdraw and hide. Aloof cats may become more loving, but in a few days, most infected animals become irritable and dangerously aggressive. Animals in this "mad dog" stage often act frenzied and deranged and will attack viciously without provocation. In the dumb phase, paralysis overtakes the body, starting with the face, jaw, and throat muscles.

Unable to swallow his own saliva, the afflicted feline may foam at the mouth or, more typically, drool saliva that looks like strings of egg white. Eventually, the rear legs give way, and the cat can no longer stand or walk. Death soon follows.

Fortunately, regular vaccination easily prevents this merciless disease. Because of the threat to human health, the rabies vaccine is a core part of every cat's immunization program. In addition, most localities have laws requiring immunization of dogs and cats. To guarantee a certain immunity level, an initial rabies vaccine requires a booster one year later. Thereafter, some areas permit boosters that do not need to be repeated again for three years, depending on the type of vaccine given.

Without question, all outdoor cats should be immunized against rabies because of their potential exposure to infected animals, wild or domestic. Even if your cat stays indoors, keep his rabies immunization current in case the cat bites someone or in case he escapes outdoors and risks exposure to a rabid animal. If your cat bites someone, certain quarantine procedures may apply, and you will certainly need legal proof of current immunization from your veterinarian.

Feline Leukemia Virus (FeLV)

First discovered in 1964, FeLV belongs to a special family of viruses called retroviruses. FeLV suppresses the bone marrow and the immune system, rendering its victims vulnerable to various cancers, such as leukemia, and other secondary ailments. Symptoms vary but generally include weight loss, anemia, poor appetite, lethargy, and recurring infections. An infected cat may seem healthy for years before finally succumbing to an FeLV-related illness. Testing is available to determine FeLV status with reasonable accuracy, although an occasional false positive or false negative result is possible. To help prevent the spread of the disease, all cats should be tested to ensure their negative status before being introduced into a new household with other felines.

Cats allowed outdoors have the highest risk of FeLV exposure and certainly should be vaccinated. Others at risk include those living in multicat households and those exposed to outdoor cats, whether through direct contact or through screened windows. To be safe, any cat that comes into contact with other cats through breeding programs, at boarding kennels, or at cat shows needs protection against FeLV. Breeding toms and queens should be tested and certified free of the virus. Ideally, kittens should be tested before vaccination to rule out disease, because they can acquire the virus from an infected mother through the placenta or through the breast milk. If FeLV-positive, vaccination likely will neither help nor harm them.

Because the disease passes from cat to cat through bite wounds and prolonged casual contact, all FeLV-

positive cats should be kept indoors and isolated from FeLV-negative cats, even vaccinated ones. There is no evidence to indicate that FeLV is capable of causing disease in people.

Feline Infectious Peritonitis (FIP)

This potentially fatal illness is caused by a coronavirus that spurs an inflammatory reaction in the blood vessels and body tissues. The disease strikes primarily younger and older cats and those debilitated by other illnesses, such as feline leukemia virus. Common signs include fever, lethargy, appetite and weight loss, and an overall unthrifty appearance. FIP typically takes one of two forms, wet or dry. The wet form involves fluid buildup in the abdomen and chest. An afflicted cat exhibits labored breathing, extreme depression, and a swollen belly. The dry form progresses more slowly and affects many organs, including the liver, kidneys, pancreas, brain, and eyes. Because symptoms are often vague, the dry form is more difficult to diagnose. The first FIP vaccine became available in 1991 and is given in the form of nose drops. Many veterinarians recommend it only if the exposure threat is high. The disease poses a greater hazard in catteries and multicat households, so discuss this vaccine option with your veterinarian.

Feline Immunodeficiency Virus (FIV)

Discovered in 1987, FIV is a retrovirus in the same family as FeLV and human immunodeficiency virus (HIV), the virus that causes AIDS. Although FIV is sometimes called feline *AIDS*, it is important to understand that people *cannot* catch this disease from cats. FIV is a species-specific virus, meaning that it infects only cats and is not transmissible to humans or to other animal species.

The disease appears to be transmitted among cats mainly through bites. Because they often engage in territorial fighting, free-roaming males have the highest risk of contracting FIV. Cats kept indoors have the least risk, which is another sound reason to keep your feline companion safely inside.

A test can confirm a cat's FIV status as positive or negative, although no cure exists. Once contracted, the disease persists for life, although a cat may remain healthy for months or years before his immune system weakens enough to allow secondary infections to take hold. Symptoms vary but usually include lethargy, weight loss, gum disease, and chronic infections. A vaccine is available. Prevention also involves avoiding contact with potentially infected cats, which is easily accomplished by keeping your cat indoors. Also, it's a good idea to have all breeding animals and all new cats coming into your household tested for FIV (and FeLV) to ensure their negative status, before exposing them to your cat.

Feline Lower Urinary Tract Disease (FLUTD)

The urinary tract collects and disposes of urine through the bladder and a tube called the urethra. In female cats, the urethra is short and wide; in males, this opening through which urine passes is longer and more narrow. For this reason, males are more prone to urinary tract blockages than females, although problems can occur in both sexes. In FLUTD, also called feline urologic syndrome or simply FUS, tiny mineral crystals form in the lower urinary tract and irritate the internal tissues.

In response to this discomfort, the cat may repeatedly lick its penis or vulva and urinate in unusual places, such as the bathtub. Feeling an uncomfortable urgency to urinate, the cat may make frequent trips to the litter box. The cat even may strain or cry as he attempts to void. Some people mistake this straining to urinate for constipation. If you notice these symptoms, or if you see blood in the urine, take your cat to a veterinarian immediately. If the crystals are large enough, they may block the urethra completely, creating a life-threatening emergency. If the cat cannot eliminate his urine, the kidneys may sustain irreversible damage from the backup pressure and within a short time, toxic wastes can build up in the blood with fatal consequences. With

prompt medical treatment, most cats recover; however, recurrences are common. Often, bacterial infections in the bladder or urethra complicate matters. The veterinarian may recommend medications and dietary changes to manage the condition.

While dietary factors are known to play an influential role in the disorder (see page 72), some veterinarians believe that disruptive and drastic changes in the environment or the household routine may detrimentally influence urinary tract health as well.

Internal Parasites

While many internal parasites can afflict the cat, the most common include tapeworms, roundworms, and hookworms. An infected queen can pass certain worms to her kittens through the placenta and through the breast milk; therefore, during your cat's first visit to the veterinarian, request a stool analysis, which unveils the presence of most worms. Because deworming drugs can cause toxic reactions, they should be

Quick Reference Chart

Internal Parasites	Symptoms	Mode of Transmission
Tapeworms: Appropriate flea control measures are preventive	Fresh segments passed in stool look like white, wriggling grains of rice	Rodents and fleas; cats ingest fleas during self-grooming; larvae mature inside cat's intestines
Roundworms	Vomiting, diarrhea, weight loss, potbelly, overall poor condition, white, spaghetti-like strands may be visible in vomit or stool	Contact with contaminated cat feces; kittens may contract from infected mothers
Hookworms	Anemia, diarrhea, weight loss, black, tarry stools	Larvae-infested soil; more prevalent in hot, humid areas
Heartworms: Preventive medication recommended in high-risk regions	Shortness of breath, coughing, periodic vomiting	Mosquito bites; more prevalent in humid, mosquito-plagued regions
Lungworms	Dry, persistent cough	Contact with infected cats; eating infected birds or rodents
Giardia: A protozoan parasite that causes an intestinal infection, giardiasis, in adult cats	Recurrent diarrhea; stools may be yellowish and foamy, often varying from soft to normal; overall unthrifty appearance	Drinking water that has been contaminated with fecal matter containing the organism's cysts

administered only under veterinary supervision.

An effective parasite prevention program includes keeping cats indoors, getting regular veterinary checkups, maintaining good sanitation, and controlling fleas, rodents, and other vermin. Cats allowed outdoors should be checked for internal parasites during their annual physical checkups.

Tapeworms

The most common internal parasites found in adult cats, tapeworms are transmitted by rodents and fleas. During grooming, cats ingest fleas, which often carry immature tapeworms. Once ingested, the tapeworm larvae mature inside the cat's intestines, feeding on nutrients within and growing into long, segmented strands. When passed in the stool, fresh tapeworm segments look like grains of white rice and, upon close inspection, may even be wriggling. Occasionally, dried segments that look like tiny, flat seeds may be observed sticking to the hair around the cat's anus. Left untreated, tapeworms rarely cause any outward clinical signs, but because they feed on the intestinal contents, they can rob the cat of important nutrients. For effective treatment, combine deworming agents with appropriate flea control measures.

Roundworms

Kittens get roundworms from their infected mothers or through contact with contaminated cat feces. Signs of parasitic infestation may include vomiting, diarrhea, weight loss, a potbellied appearance, and overall poor condition. Roundworms passed in vomit or stool look like white, wriggling spaghetti strands.

Hookworms

More prevalent in hot, humid areas, hookworms are picked up from soil infested with the larvae. Symptoms may include anemia, diarrhea, weight loss, and black, tarry stools.

Heartworms

Heartworms also occur in cats, particularly in humid regions, but they more commonly affect the dog. However, the incidence of this condition in cats appears to be on the rise, especially in certain high-risk areas where the mosquito, the host organism for heartworm disease, strongly prevails. Cats acquire the disease from the bite of a larvae-carrying mosquito. The larvae migrate to the cat's heart and pulmonary arteries, where they mature into adult worms. In most cases, a cat's normally functioning immune system mounts an attack and kills the larvae before they reach the heart. However, if one parasite survives to adulthood inside the cat, the cat may develop shortness of breath, coughing, and periodic vomiting. Once a cat is infected with heartworms, treatment can be risky. The medication used to kill adult worms can have serious side effects, so prevention is a much better choice.

If you live in a humid, mosquito-plagued region, your veterinarian may recommend preventive heartworm medication for your cat, so be sure to discuss this option during your cat's regular checkup.

Lungworms

Acquired from contact with infected cats or from eating infected birds and rodents, lungworms migrate to a cat's lungs and cause a dry, persistent cough.

Flukes

Although uncommon, flukes can be ingested by eating infected raw fish and other small prey.

Giardia

Cats that began life outdoors or that live outside may contract a protozoan parasite that can cause an intestinal infection called giardiasis. The most notable symptom is recurrent diarrhea. Stools may be yellowish and foamy, often varying from soft to normal. The cat may have an overall unthrifty appearance and difficulty maintaining weight. Cats acquire the parasite from drinking water that has been contaminated with fecal matter containing the organism's cysts. The infection is treatable, but it can be difficult to diagnose.

Bot Fly Larvae

Until recently, veterinarians had no clue as to the cause of an unusual and deadly neurological disorder called Feline Ischemic Encephalopathy (FIE). This puzzling disease has been around for years but, until

recently, has not been well understood. Symptoms often include sudden and profound behavioral changes, such as marked aggression or unexplained lethargy. Neurological signs may include blindness, seizures, and walking in circles. Researchers now believe that the disease is caused by the microscopic larvae of the bot fly, an insect that reproduces primarily in late summer. Cats contract the bot fly larvae from rodents and other small mammals. Initial bot fly infection may involve lumps under the skin. However, the larvae may migrate to the brain, where they cause the deadly lesions that lead to the severe neurological symptoms described above. At this time, no cure or proven treatment exists for FIE, and diagnosis can be difficult and expensive. Most cats that contract the parasitic ailment are euthanized, and those that survive usually sustain lasting neurological damage. To date, the best prevention is simply to keep your cat safely indoors at all times, especially during the late summer months (July through September), where your pet has little opportunity of coming into contact with bot fly larvae.

External Parasites

Fleas

Fleas, without question, are the most common external parasites to plague cats and frustrate their owners. Easy to spot, these annoying insects leave behind evidence of their visits to the host in the form of flea dirt, which looks like fine grains of black sand in the cat's fur. To inspect for flea dirt, rub your hand against your cat's fur along his back, and near the neck and tail, and look closely at the skin for tiny black specks. Fleas feed on the cat's blood, which means the pepperlike granules deposited in the fur are

really flea excrement from digested blood. If dampened, the tiny specks dissolve into bloody smudges. Left untreated, flea infestations can cause anemia from blood loss, especially in kittens, and damage a cat's coat and skin from excessive scratching.

Even indoor cats are not immune to the scourge of fleas. Following the mere scent of a warm-blooded animal, these tiny but relentlessly bloodthirsty and biting insects can jump through holes in walls or window screens or ride in on a person's clothing or shoes in search of a suitable host. Once indoors, fleas lay eggs on the host and turn your cat's plush, dense fur into a virtual nursery for millions more. As the cat moves and scratches, the eggs fall off into your carpets, upholstery, and bedding, where they hatch into larvae. The larvae feed on debris among deep carpet fibers, an indoor environment that mimics their natural habitat, grass. Frequent vacuuming helps control this stage, but throw out the bag afterward, or the larvae will simply mature inside the bag and jump out.

Flea control: Effective flea control used to require an expensive arsenal of products designed to treat the pet and its environment at various phases of the flea's complex life cycle. This arsenal included sprays, dips, powders, flea collars, medicated shampoos, and room foggers, all targeted to kill or control fleas at the egg, larval, pupal, or adult stages. Often, these products failed to be effective when applied

Quick Reference Chart

External Parasites	Symptoms	Control Measures
Fleas: Even indoor cats are commonly plagued by these tiny, biting insects that feed on blood	Excessive scratching, presence of flea dirt, tiny black specks of flea excrement that turn bloody when dampened, in the fur	Effective one-spot, once-a-month flea control medications are available through veterinarians
Ticks: some ticks carry Lyme disease, which humans can catch	Felt as a bump in the cat's fur after tick burrows head into skin and swells from sucking blood	Remove tick promptly by grasping and pulling straight out with tweezers; wear rubber gloves
Lice: Uncommon in well-kept, healthy cats	White specks (nits) stuck to fur	Clip coat and bathe cat with medicated shampoo available through veterinarians
Mites: Most common variety found in the cat is the ear mite, which burrows in the ear canal and can cause ear infection	Itchiness, hair loss, crusty sores, scaly dandruff, body odor, ear mites: crumbly, waxy, brown buildup in ears, head shaking; scratching at ears, holding ears to side of head, staggering	Veterinarian must identify specific mite variety before dispensing appropriate medication; other cats and dogs in household may require treatment also, due to contagion
Ringworm: Not a worm at all but a fungus; prompt treatment is required, as infection can spread from cats to humans	Itchiness, scaly skin, patchy hair loss	Clip coat, bathe cat, disinfect pet bedding, administer medications as recommended by a veterinarian; a noncore vaccine is preventive in high-risk households where ringworm has been a past problem

during the wrong life cycle of the insect and required repeating. They could also be potentially dangerous if used inappropriately or in combination with incompatible products. Even flea collars, although easy to use, posed a risk of strangling or choking, unless designed with elastic or breakaway sections to make them safer.

Once-a-month products: Fortunately, flea control is now much eas-

Parasite Control

Ask your veterinarian to recommend an appropriate flea and parasite control for your cat, as there are many products to choose from and new ones coming on the market all the time. Several factors must be considered, including your cat's age, lifestyle, and overall health, as well as your willingness and ability to administer the product.

ier and more effective with the use of one-spot products that are applied topically once a month. One such product is Advantage (imidacloprid). It comes in a small tube and is dabbed directly onto the cat's skin at the back of the neck once a month. A similar topical product applied in the same fashion is Frontline Top Spot (fipronil) for cats. The active ingredient in both products

spreads across the entire animal and kills adult fleas by impairing the insects' nervous system, before they can lay eggs and before they can bite and irritate the cat.

Some newer topical agents provide protection against more than just fleas. One of these is Revolution (selamectin) for cats, which is also a topical product applied once a month. Revolution kills fleas by blocking nerve signal transmissions. It can also kill certain intestinal parasites, ear mites, and ticks, and helps prevent heartworm disease.

Oral products: An oral once-a-month product called PROGRAM (lufenuron) is taken internally and must be mixed in the cat's food. For this drug to work, fleas must bite the host and drink its blood. Once they feast on the cat's treated blood, female fleas living on the host will produce infertile eggs. Male fleas are unaffected. By interfering with the flea's reproductive cycle, the drug is useful for controlling indoor infestations. However, because of the way the drug must work, it is no cure-all for cats that suffer from flea allergy dermatitis (see page 128), an allergic reaction to flea bites.

Although the once-a-month products tend to be somewhat expensive, they pay for themselves in terms of effectiveness, convenience, and ease of application. They spare you the hassle and your cat the trauma of repeated dips, baths, powderings, and sprayings.

What to look for on a product label: When choosing and using any

type of flea control product, remember these important rules:

• Select only products labeled *safe for use on cats.* Products intended for use only on dogs often contain medications that are too strong, sometimes even fatal, when applied to cats.

• Read the product label directions carefully *before* using the product on your cat. If you have questions, don't guess. Call your veterinarian and clarify any concerns you may have about using the product.

• Never use any product on a kitten or a debilitated cat without veterinary approval.

• Be careful to avoid potentially toxic combinations. Some products do not mix and match well, so before using more than one flea control product, or before using any product with other medications your cat may be taking, ask your veterinarian if the ingredients can be used together safely.

Ticks

Besides fleas, cats sometimes play host to ticks, lice, and mites. Ticks burrow their heads into the skin and suck blood. They often go unnoticed until they swell large enough to be felt as a bump in the cat's fur. If you discover one, remove it promptly by grasping the tick's body as close to the cat's skin as possible with tweezers.

Note: Because of the risks to human health, experts recommend wearing rubber gloves while removing ticks, and thoroughly washing your hands afterward.

Pull the tick straight out (without twisting) with firm, gentle traction, then drown the insect in alcohol. Make sure you've extracted the entire insect, head and all; otherwise, a piece left behind may cause an infection under the skin, requiring veterinary attention.

Because some ticks carry diseases, such as Lyme disease, that can affect humans, take precautions to check for and control these external parasites, if you choose to allow your cat to go outdoors. A tick can manage to hitch a ride even when its host experiences only short forays into the grass. Some products used to control fleas also repel or kill ticks, so ask your veterinarian to recommend one.

Lice

Uncommon in well-kept, healthy cats, lice look like white specks (nits) stuck to the fur. Clipping the coat and bathing with a medicated shampoo, available through veterinarians, gets rid of them.

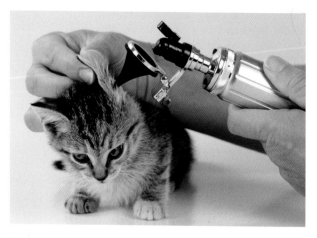

Mites

Being microscopic, mites are hard to see, but signs of their presence include itchiness, hair loss, crusty sores, scaly dandruff, and body odor. Before recommending appropriate treatment, a veterinarian needs to identify the specific mite variety through examination.

Ear mites: The most common mite found on cats is the ear mite, which lives in the ear canal and produces a crumbly, dark brown, foul-smelling, waxy discharge. While healthy ears are clean and pink inside, a waxy, brown buildup in your cat's ears may indicate ear mites. Other signs include head shaking, holding the ears to the side of the head, and repeatedly scratching at the ears. Prompt treatment prevents spread to the inner ear, where an infection can lead to hearing impairment. Symptoms of inner ear infection, such as staggering and loss of balance, require immediate medical attention. Because ear mites are contagious, other cats and dogs in the household may need treatment as well.

Ringworm

This skin disorder is not caused by a worm at all, but rather by a fungus. Signs include scaly skin and patchy hair loss. Because people can catch this skin infection from cats, prompt veterinary treatment and disinfection of pet bedding are essential. Treatment may include clipping the coat, bathing the skin, and administering topical or oral medications. An optional vaccine is available to prevent ringworm, but veterinarians generally recommend it only if exposure risk is high, as in households where ringworm has been a past problem. Discuss this option with your veterinarian, if it is a concern.

Feline Vital Signs

Taking a cat's temperature is a procedure few felines relish or submit to readily. While this chore is best left to your veterinarian, sometimes it may be necessary for you to do it yourself so you can report the vital signs to your veterinarian. And even if you never need to do the deed, it's good to know what normal vital signs are in the cat.

Temperature: Normal body temperature in cats ranges from 100 to 102.5°F (37.8–39°C), with the average being about 101.5°F (38.6°C). Any temperature higher than 102.5°F (39°C) is cause for concern. To take a cat's temperature, use a plastic digital rectal thermometer designed either for pets or for human infants. If using a rectal thermometer is a turnoff to you, there are ear thermometers for pets that work by measuring infrared heat waves coming from the ear, but these generally require some practice to get accurate readings.

To take a cat's temperature rectally, you likely will need someone to help you restrain and reassure the cat. One convenient means of restraint is to wrap a towel around the cat, leaving the head and rear exposed. Then lubricate the thermometer with petroleum jelly (Vaseline), lift the cat's tail, and gently insert the thermometer into the anus about an inch (2.5 cm). Hold it in place for one or two minutes, or until the digital thermometer beeps.

Pulse and respiration: To take a cat's pulse, feel for it high up on the inside hind leg. Normal pulse rate ranges from 100 to 180 beats per minute. Normal respiration is 20 to 30 breaths per minute. Ask your veterinarian to show you how to take these vital signs.

Allergies in Cats

Like people, cats can develop allergies to a host of things in their environment, such as pollen, weeds, grasses, mold spores, house dust, feathers, wool, insect stings, drugs, chemicals, and food ingredients, but instead of sneezing, watery eyes, and runny noses, cats' symptoms more likely involve itchy skin, face, and ears. Typical warning signs include compulsive rubbing against furniture or carpet and excessive scratching, licking, or chewing at itchy places. Gastrointestinal symptoms such as vomiting and diarrhea also can occur, particularly if the allergen, or allergy-causing substance, is ingested in a food or drug. Redness, crusty skin, and hair loss around the nose, mouth, and face suggest a food allergy, or possibly an allergy to plas-

By far the most common allergy condition seen in cats is an uncomfortable and unsightly skin condition called flea allergy dermatitis. It is caused by an oversensitivity to flea bites, or more correctly, to the saliva fleas leave behind after they bite. Some cats are so allergic to flea saliva that the bite from a single flea will send them into a frenzy, scratching, biting, and licking to get at the culprit. The severe itching lasts long after the flea feeds and departs, so you may never even see one of these nasty external parasites on your pet. Besides itchiness, other symptoms include hair loss, patchy redness (called hot spots), and scabby, crusty sores on the skin.

Treatment consists of appropriate medications dispensed by your veterinarian to relieve the itching and associated skin problems. In addition, aggressive and diligent flea control measures help lessen the condition's severity and occurrence. A preferred choice would be a topical one-spot, once-a-month flea control product that kills adult fleas before they have a chance to bite the cat (see page 123).

Feline Dental Care

Cats are not prone to getting cavities, but they are susceptible to gum disease, which can eventually lead to tooth loss. Dental disease can also silently compromise your cat's immune system and overall health

tic feeding dishes. In the latter case, replacing plastic dishes with lead-free ceramic or stainless steel ones offers an easy remedy.

Unfortunately, many allergy cases in the cat are not so simple to solve or control. Testing exists, but allergies remain difficult to diagnose. Treatment varies widely from patient to patient, depending on the cause and symptoms, and may include antihistamines or allergy shots. Recovery can take a long time, and because allergies usually persist for a lifetime, owners must commit to avoiding or reducing the allergen in the cat's environment for as long as the animal lives.

by allowing bacteria to leak into the bloodstream from pockets of pus around sore, infected gums. Normal, healthy gums are pink, but diseased gums are tender, red, and swollen— signs of gingivitis (inflamed gums) caused by plaque and tartar buildup. Left untreated, this condition causes the gums to recede gradually and the teeth to loosen.

Bad breath is a cardinal sign of dental disease, but a cat with dental problems may also have difficulty eating because his teeth and gums hurt. As a result, he may lose weight and condition. A cat with sensitive teeth also may flinch when you try to stroke the side of his face. The best way to prevent such discomfort is to regularly brush or rinse your cat's teeth with oral hygiene products designed for use in animals. Also, from time to time, you may need to have your cat's teeth professionally cleaned. For this procedure, the cat is anesthetized, and the veterinarian uses an ultrasonic scaler to blast away the ugly, brown tartar and polish the teeth.

Brushing a Cat's Teeth

Cats are not the most cooperative creatures when it comes to having their teeth inspected or their mouths handled. Getting them to submit to toothbrushing requires great patience and gentleness. Some steadfastly refuse to cooperate from the outset. To have any chance of success, you need to introduce cats to the idea early, while they are still kittens. While it's not impossible to train an adult cat

to tolerate toothbrushing, doing so takes more time; an older cat may never fully accept the procedure without a fuss. But the payoffs for your efforts, if successful, are worthwhile. Your cat will have healthier gums, which may help contribute to a longer life. Your cat also may be able to go longer between professional teeth cleanings, which helps you avoid subjecting him to the inherent risks associated with anesthesia and the repeated costs of such procedures.

To begin your at-home dental care routine, ask your veterinarian to show you how to take care of your cat's teeth. Some veterinary clinics have how-to videos on the subject to show their clients. Your veterinarian also can recommend an appropriate mouth rinse or a non-foaming, enzymatic toothpaste made especially for animals. These pastes, designed to dissolve plaque without a lot of scrubbing action,

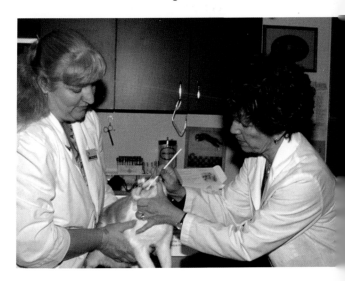

come in fish, poultry, and malt flavors for finicky felines.

Then, visit your local pet store and purchase a small pet toothbrush with ultra-soft bristles. Some pet toothbrushes are designed as soft rubber or plastic tips that fit over your finger. Most people who've tried this type say they are easier to use on cats than regular toothbrushes with handles. While you can use a soft, worn-out human toothbrush on pets, *never* use human toothpaste, because it will burn the back of your cat's throat and, if swallowed, can cause stomach upset.

To begin training your cat to accept the idea of having his teeth brushed, dip your finger in something tasty, such as canned tuna cat food juice, and gently rub the cat's teeth and gums. After about a week of doing this, try using the brush on

only a few teeth on one side of the mouth. If your cat doesn't accept the brush right away, wrap gauze around your finger and gently massage the teeth and gums. With each try, clean a few more teeth, until your cat gradually accepts the process without a fuss. If the cat struggles, don't force him to submit. Instead, be extra gentle and patient, so he won't learn to dread having his mouth handled. Offer lots of praise and a tasty treat afterward.

Dental care aids: For cats that refuse to submit to the indignity of toothbrushing, you can try several alternative dental care aids on the market. Tartar control treats, plaque control products, dental foods, and enzymatic chews, while not a substitute for brushing, can help. Ask your veterinarian about them and discuss how your cat's routine dental care should be handled.

Medicating Your Cat

Getting your cat used to having his mouth opened and handled will make it much easier for you to give him oral medications, should the need arise. Otherwise, the ordeal is likely to be a two-person job, with

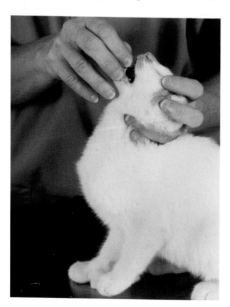

To give a cat a pill, grasp the head gently with one hand, placing your thumb and index finger on the cat's cheekbones. Tilt the head back slightly, then gently pry open the jaws with the other hand. Drop the pill as far back in the throat as possible.

one person holding the cat while the other administers the medicine. Giving pills and liquids are covered here because they are the most common forms of medication you will likely have to administer. But whether your cat's condition calls for oral medications, injections, eye ointments, ear drops, or force-feeding that you must do at home, ask your veterinarian to explain and demonstrate the best method of application and safe restraint. Make sure you understand how and when to administer any medication before you attempt to do it yourself, and know what to expect in terms of recovery time and side effects.

Never give your cat any drug or over-the-counter painkillers meant for humans. Products that contain acetaminophen are especially deadly to cats, even in small amounts. Aspirin products can also be lethal to cats. While certain products made for humans can be used on cats, the dosage, in many cases, must be diluted or carefully controlled and monitored. So never try to medicate your cat with herbal remedies, over-the-counter medications, or any other product not specifically labeled as safe for use on cats without seeking veterinary advice first.

Restraint Methods

Medicating a cat is best carried out in quiet surroundings with minimal physical restraint. Often, however, the task turns into a two-person job: one to hold the cat and one to administer the medication. One way to restrain an uncooperative cat is to wrap his body in a large towel, leaving only the head sticking out. This gives you some protection from claws. Many pet stores carry cat restraint bags that zip up and enclose the cat with only the head exposed for breathing, but a pillowcase or coat sleeve work just as well.

Another common method is to grasp the cat by the scruff or nape of the neck and hold it down on a table. Most cats go limp when you do this, much like when their mothers carried them as kittens. However, do *not* lift an adult cat by the scruff of the neck without supporting the hind feet with your arm. Without support, you risk injuring the cat's neck muscles.

Pills: To give a cat a pill, grasp the cat's head with your thumb and

detect medications added to their food and usually eat around the edges or refuse the food altogether. Sometimes, lacing the drug with tuna oil or concealing it in strong-smelling, fish-flavored canned food works. When adding medication to food, make sure your other animals do not consume it.

Preventing Hair Balls

Cats, especially longhaired ones, can swallow a lot of loose hair as they groom themselves, particularly at the height of shedding season. Normally, this creates no problem. The hair simply moves through the digestive tract and gets eliminated in the usual way. Occasionally, however, too much hair accumulates in the stomach and is vomited back up as a hair ball. In more serious cases, the hair may form a large mass further along in the digestive tract, causing a blockage and requiring an enema or even surgery to remove. Signs of a blockage include refusal to eat or regurgitating food shortly after eating.

The term *hair ball* is sort of a misnomer, because hair balls aren't round or ball-shaped at all. They are, in fact, soft, tubular masses of ingested hair. Just before a cat spits up a hair ball, it will crouch low and cough a few times in a dry, hacking, wheezing manner. Sometimes the cat will sway his head from side to

index finger on his cheekbones and tilt back the head. With the forefinger of your other hand, gently pry open the jaws, then drop the pill as far back into the back of the throat as possible. Hold the cat's mouth shut with one hand and stroke his throat with your other. The stroking motion encourages the cat to swallow.

Liquids: To administer liquid medication, tilt the cat's head back slightly, insert an eyedropper or syringe (without needle) into the corner of the mouth, and gently squeeze in a few drops at a time, allowing the cat time to swallow. Do not squirt the medication into the cat's mouth too quickly or too forcefully, because the cat may accidentally inhale the liquid into the lungs, which could lead to pneumonia. Hold the animal's mouth shut and stroke the throat until the cat swallows.

Some liquid medications can be mixed in the cat's food if they are not too bitter tasting. Cats can easily side as he coughs. This is distinctly recognized as the hair ball cough. As the cat prepares to vomit, he will crouch and convulse his whole body in waves before ejecting the material onto the floor. Except for the mess, vomiting a hair ball is usually no cause for concern, unless it becomes too frequent, in which case you need to offer some remedy.

As one might guess, hair balls are generally more of a problem in long-haired cats than in shorthaired cats. Regular grooming is the easiest and cheapest way to prevent hair balls. Brushing and combing your cat helps remove the loose, dead hair he would otherwise swallow.

Remedies

Should you happen to find spit-up hair balls on your carpet, or if you see your cat crouching and displaying the typical hair ball cough without results, remedies are available. These include several petrolatum-based hair ball pastes available through veterinarians or at pet supply stores. Typically, these products come in a tube. To administer, you squeeze a ribbon of paste onto your finger and entice the cat to lick it, or you place an amount on the cat's tongue or paw. Another option is to dab some plain nonmedicated petroleum jelly (Vaseline) on the top part of your cat's front paw to lick off. These products help lubricate the hair mass so that it is expelled more easily.

Grass also seems to act as a purgative to help cats expel excess hair from the stomach. You can grow a fresh supply of grass indoors for your cat, and most pet stores sell kitty grass kits specifically for this purpose. Most cats love to nibble on greenery, and providing yours with his own personal supply may also help keep him from devouring your houseplants.

Recently, at least one specialty food product formulated for hair ball control has appeared on the cat food market. Such foods contain natural vegetable fiber, which provides roughage and helps keep things moving along through the intestinal tract. Cat treats specially formulated to treat hair balls are available from veterinarians, too.

Feline First Aid

Cats often conceal illness or pain, but observant owners can detect subtle behavior changes that cue them that all is not well. Early injury and disease detection can greatly enhance the odds of full recovery. Set aside time once a week to assess your cat's overall condition. Make a practice of inspecting your cat for white teeth, pink gums, clean, pink ears, clear, bright eyes free of discharge, clean fur free of flea dirt, and a firm body free of lumps, bumps, and tender spots. By doing so regularly, you are more apt to notice anything out of the ordinary.

Once recognized, the key to successfully coping with any emergency is to be prepared for it. Always keep

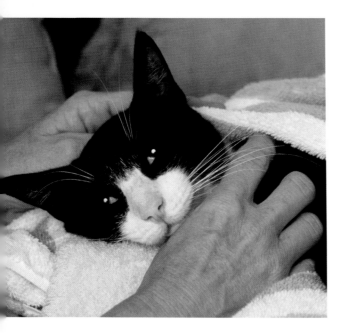

Bleeding: If an injured cat loses too much blood, he may go into shock and die before you reach a veterinary clinic. To control bleeding, cover visible wounds with gauze pads or some clean material and apply gentle, direct pressure over the site for several minutes. Do not attempt to splint or straighten fractured limbs, as this could cause more damage if done improperly.

Transporting the Cat to a Veterinary Clinic: Never pick up an injured animal by placing your hands under the belly. This will only worsen chest or abdominal injuries. If the cat is lying down, approach him from behind, slide one hand under the chest and one hand under the rump, and gently place him in a pet carrier or on a blanket for transport. If the cat is crouched, grasp the scruff of the neck with one hand, place the other hand under the hips and rear legs for support, and cradle the cat in your arms. If the cat struggles, wrap him in a large towel or blanket, leaving only the head sticking out. (See page 131 for restraint methods.) Remember, no matter how gentle your cat is, he may bite or claw you if he's in pain. Protect your hands with gloves and wear long sleeves.

Heatstroke or Frostbite: Heatstroke and frostbite require immediate medical attention. To prevent frostbite, keep your cat indoors and avoid overexposure during cold weather. To prevent heatstroke, *never* leave your cat in a parked car, not even for a few minutes, not even with the windows cracked. Temperatures inside a car

your veterinarian's emergency number handy. In addition, assemble the following items in a first-aid kit:
• A blanket or towel to wrap your cat in for warmth and safe restraint
• Gauze pads and strips for bandaging
• Hydrogen peroxide antiseptic (it's fresh only if it bubbles) to clean wounds and induce vomiting
• Antibiotic ointment, such as Neosporin, for superficial wounds
• Tweezers, handy for removing foreign objects from paw pads or from the throat, if the cat is choking
• Waterproof pouch to hold ice for controlling swelling and bleeding
• Scissors and adhesive tape
• Artificial tears or sterile saline eye rinse to flush foreign material from eyes
• Rectal thermometer, pediatric size

rapidly climb too high for safe tolerance, even on mild days, and with only hot air to breathe, your cat can quickly suffer brain damage and die from heatstroke. Signs of heat stress include panting, vomiting, glazed eyes, rapid pulse, staggering, and red or purple tongue. Cool the body with tepid water, wrap in wet towels, and transport to a veterinary clinic immediately.

Accidental Poisoning

If you suspect your cat has ingested a potentially hazardous substance, call your veterinarian immediately. Do not induce vomiting unless an expert advises it. Some substances can cause more harm when vomited back up. When advised to induce vomiting, administer a small amount of hydrogen peroxide or warm salt water by mouth with an eyedropper. If you know what poisonous substance was ingested, take the package or a sample with you to the veterinarian.

For 24-hour assistance, seven days a week, call the ASPCA Animal Poison Control Information Center. The hotline number is (888) 426-4435. The service charges a fee, payable by credit card.

Certain medications and flea products cause some cats to salivate a little immediately after application. In many cases, this is no cause for concern, and the reaction subsides after a minute or two. However, if your cat begins salivat-

Wrap your injured cat in a towel or blanket to restrain him.

ing *heavily* after you've applied a topical flea preparation to his fur, or if he staggers or shows other unusual signs, rinse the substance off right away and call your veterinarian. Don't use the product on your cat again.

Similarly, if your cat's coat or paws become contaminated by bleach, pesticides, paint products, household cleaners and disinfectants, oil, tar, antifreeze, or other potential poisons, wash off the offending substance immediately. If necessary, clip away the affected fur. If the coat appears to be heavily saturated, or if you believe the cat may have already licked some of the substance from its coat or paws, seek veterinary help.

Foreign Objects

If the cat is salivating, gagging, and pawing at his mouth, he may be choking on a foreign object in his mouth. Frequent culprits are bones, toothpicks, or staples stuck between the upper back teeth. Cats in this predicament often become quite frantic and, in their frenzied state, may claw or bite anyone who tries to help them. Transporting the animal to a nearby veterinary clinic for emergency assistance is usually the best approach, but if you feel you can do so safely, attempt to open the mouth and gently pull back the tongue for a better view down the throat. If you can see an obstructing object, use tweezers to gently extract it. If the object does not readily dislodge, make no further attempt to remove it without veterinary help—you may do more harm than good. Never poke tweezers into the eyes or ears; foreign objects lodged in these areas are best removed by a professional.

Euthanasia and Pet Loss

The unfortunate part of pet ownership is that cats don't live as long as people do. The average life span for a cat is about 10 to 15 years, although many cats are living longer, thanks to improved nutrition and modern veterinary care. Eventually, however, all cat owners have to let go of their devoted companions and say good-bye.

Although difficult and painful, the decision to euthanize (humanely put to death) a cat is sometimes the last and kindest gift an owner can offer a longtime companion suffering or debilitated from illness, injury, or old age. An anesthetic overdose administered by a veterinarian simply puts the cat to sleep without pain. Some veterinarians allow owners who request it to remain with the cat during the brief procedure, and many help handle cremation or burial arrangements.

For many people, losing a cherished cat companion causes as much trauma and heartbreak as losing a human loved one. This is not surprising, since the grieving process for pets is essentially the same as it is when we lose a human partner. The loss is especially intense when our pets have shared our daily lives more closely than our relatives or human friends.

Unfortunately, some people simply don't understand how much it hurts to lose an animal friend. These unenlightened folks may make well-meaning but misguided comments, such as, "It was only a cat. Just get another one!" These comments belittle the special bond you had with your cat—don't listen to them. Instead, talk to people who understand your grief. Find out if your area has pet grief counseling and support groups to help people through this crisis. Ask your veterinarian for details.

When the inevitable does happen, giving another cat a good home is a beautiful way to honor your deceased friend's memory. Some people want to get another cat right away, while others feel a need to let some time pass. There is no single best way to handle the pain of loss. Just do what feels right for you. Another cat will not replace the one you lost, but when you feel ready, you can build a new relationship with another cat that will be as uniquely special, joyful, and rewarding.

Chapter Seven

Grooming Your Cat

The Purpose of Fur

Fur serves to protect and insulate the cat from the elements. Generally speaking, a cat's coat consists of a topcoat of guard hairs over a soft undercoat of down and awn hairs. The coarser guard hairs protect the undercoat from the elements, the soft down hairs closest to the skin provide added warmth, while the awn hairs form a middle layer of insulation. The guard and awn hairs also can fluff out to trap air for better insulation. Depending on the breed, not all cats have all three types of hairs, and not all cats have hair. The Sphynx, for example, is a hairless breed, even though a sparse layer of fine, soft down covers some of these animals.

The general condition of the coat serves as a good indicator of your cat's overall health. For instance, you'll want to schedule a visit to the veterinarian if you notice that your cat's skin is looking dry or flaky, or if the coat appears dull, looks oily, smells bad, or feels brittle. Several medical and dietary problems can affect the skin and coat, including allergies, parasites, and hormonal or nutritional imbalances, among others.

Benefits of Grooming

If you make grooming a habit, you'll be much more likely to notice certain problems with your cat, such as concealed cuts, scratches, lumps, or bumps that may warrant veterinary investigation, or even a hidden tick that has latched on for a blood meal. Regular grooming is also essential to control shedding and keep your cat's coat looking nice. Brushing helps stimulate circulation and distribute natural oils through the coat, keeping the fur shiny and healthy looking.

For a shorthaired cat, one 10-minute beauty session a week is usually sufficient. But if your cat has long hair, you may need to comb the coat daily, or at least several times a week, depending on the type of longhaired cat you have. Some longhaired cats have very long, fine hair, while others have medium-length fur with a coarser, silkier texture that is more resistant to matting. The undercoat makes a difference, too. Certain longhaired breeds, such as the Persian and Himalayan, are high maintenance when it comes to grooming, requiring daily combing and brushing to keep the coat ship-shape for show. These cats have a dense undercoat of fine hair, and as the animal sheds, frequent combing is a must to remove the loose, dead hairs and prevent matting. Some other longhaired breeds, such as the Turkish Angora, require less maintenance because the undercoat is not as dense.

Besides preventing mats, combing helps remove the loose cat hairs from your cat's coat before they have a chance to shed off onto your furniture. To easily wipe cat hair off your furnishings, keep a brush, lint remover, or a damp cloth handy. Combing out loose hair is also the least expensive way to prevent hairballs. Regardless of whether you intend to show, your cat's coat will need some regular attention to stay clean and mat-free.

Seasonal Shedding

Both shorthaired and longhaired cats shed during the change of seasons, from winter to spring and from summer to fall, but the process is more noticeable, particularly on your furniture, if you have a longhaired cat. Most people assume that these seasonal changes of hair coat are

caused by seasonal temperature changes, but that isn't necessarily true. Instead, experts say that environmental lighting governs the shedding process in animals.

Under natural conditions, the lengthening sunlight hours in early spring trigger the cat's body to shed hair and grow a new coat in preparation for the changing season. Similarly, autumn's shorter daylight hours cause the coat to thicken for winter. But when artificial lighting extends the daylight hours in the cat's environment year-round, this natural cycle seems to get confused. This is why house cats living in artificial lighting tend to shed a little all year.

Temperature may play a small part in the process. Overheated homes in winter appear to make some house cats prone to shed more than normal, probably because the heat tends to dry the skin.

Grooming Tools

You don't need much in the way of supplies to meet your cat's basic grooming needs.
- Invest in pet or human nail clippers, several sizes of steel pet combs, and a natural bristle brush.
- For kittens, start grooming with small and medium-size steel combs, and use a wide-toothed one on adult cats with plush, medium to long fur.
- For flea control, purchase a fine-toothed flea comb. Once caught in the comb's closely spaced teeth, fleas drown easily when dipped in a pan of water. A fine comb also readily removes flea dirt deep in the fur.

- For occasional bathing, discussed later in this chapter, you'll need a pet shampoo that is labeled as safe for use on cats.

Introduction to Grooming

Most cats love the attention they get during grooming and learn to tolerate their beauty sessions readily. If you take time to accustom your cat to the procedure early, starting at the kitten stage, and if you make each experience pleasurable, you will eventually be rewarded with not only a beautifully groomed cat, but also one that looks forward to receiving your undivided attention during these intimate, one-on-one sessions. With time and patience, the sessions can become an important human/feline bonding ritual.

Whether your cat is an adult cat or a kitten, the process of getting him accustomed to grooming is essentially the same, requiring kindness, patience, and perseverance. To begin, spend a few minutes each day gently combing your cat's fur with a metal comb, taking special care not to rake the skin with the steel teeth. Start with a small, fine-toothed comb on kitten fur, graduating to a medium- or wide-toothed comb as the cat matures.

Don't restrain your cat if his attention wanders elsewhere. Simply end the session and resume it again later. While grooming, hold the animal in your lap, or place him on a counter or table. Establish a regular grooming location and routine, and your cat will quickly learn what's expected of him when you take him to that spot and pick up the comb. Practice this routine daily for several weeks, then once your cat accepts grooming graciously, gradually decrease the number of sessions to once or twice a week.

Keep the sessions short until the cat gets used to being handled this way. Use the opportunity to get your cat accustomed to having his mouth gently opened, his ears touched, and his paws handled. This extra effort will pay off later when inspecting teeth, administering medications, cleaning ears, and trimming claws. Always end grooming sessions with a brief playtime, lots of praise and maybe even a special treat, and your cat will learn to eagerly anticipate the next one.

Combing

For convenience and versatility, some combs come with closely spaced teeth on one end and wider-spaced teeth on the other end. Use the fine-toothed end on the shorter hair around the face, head and chin. Using the wide-space end, start at the base of the neck and gently comb the back and sides. Raise the chin a little to comb the throat and chest. When combing delicate areas, such as the belly, legs, and tail, be especially careful not to rake the comb's teeth against the cat's sensitive skin.

Also, as you comb, remove any fur that may accumulate in the comb's teeth. Hair left in the comb tends to pull more hair out with it. If this pulling sensation becomes too strong, your cat will experience discomfort. Any discomfort felt during the grooming session can cause the cat to associate pain and unpleasantness with the procedure, making him an unwilling candidate the next time. So, by all means, be extra gentle and avoid pulling the hair and skin.

Using a flea comb: If you notice any flea dirt in the coat, a fine-toothed metal comb makes a dandy flea-removal instrument, handily trapping the parasites and their excrement in the closely spaced teeth. To dispatch the fleas, simply dip the comb in a nearby pan of water until the insects drown, then treat the flea problem appropriately (see pages 122–125 for information on controlling fleas).

Stripping the coat: During peak shedding periods, you may want to strip the coat of a longhaired cat occasionally by gently combing sections of fur against the way the hair lies. You can strip a plush, short-haired coat in this manner, too, but it generally isn't necessary. Called *back-combing*, this method helps remove the dead, loose hairs trapped closer to the skin as they are shed. To put the hair back in place, gently comb through it a second time, going the way the hair lies. If you intend to show your cat, you'll want to minimize stripping to keep the coat as full and plush as possible. Overstripping can make the coat look flat and thin. The majority of the time, simply comb *with* the lie of the hair, except when hair shedding is most noticeable.

Combing the tail: To add volume and fullness to a longhaired cat's tail, gently back-comb, starting at the tail base close to the body and working toward the tip. Gently fluff the tail, lifting the hair and combing upward toward the body. To avoid stripping the fragile tail hairs, use only a wide-toothed comb and remove hair from the comb as you work.

Brushing

Opinions differ widely on the best brushes to use in grooming cats. Because brush bristles can break the delicate hairs, some seasoned cat show exhibitors recommend using them sparingly, if at all. If you try using a brush, and your cat seems to prefer it to a comb, choose a soft, natural-bristle brush for the task. This will help reduce breakage and static. Use the brush as you would the comb, brushing primarily *with* the lie of the fur.

Removing Mats

While seldom a problem in short-haired cats, matting is a major concern with some longhaired cats. It is important to remove any mat right away, no matter how small. The longer one of these unsightly hair clumps remains in the coat, the tighter it pulls the skin, causing discomfort to the cat. If neglected too long, mats can irritate the skin severely enough to result in raw, open sores.

• Inspect your cat's feet periodically for mats, too. Sometimes, tiny clumps of kitty litter or other debris can get stuck on the paw pads or between the toes and become especially painful. Mats in this area probably feel a lot like having a rock in your shoe.

• Always remove any mats before bathing the cat, because water will set them permanently and make removal much more difficult.

• To remove a mat, separate the clump with your fingers and work it loose without yanking on the skin. To gently pick a stubborn mat loose, use the end teeth of a wide-toothed comb. A dab of nonmedicated grooming powder, baby oil, or hair conditioner may help loosen a tight mat, but avoid using a greasy substance unless you're planning to bathe the cat afterward.

• If the mat is a massive tangle, clipping it out with scissors, being careful not to cut the skin, or shaving it off with electric trimmers is often the last option. Pet stores sell pet clippers and mat-splitters for such grooming problems.

• A seam ripper, available at sewing supply stores, serves the same purpose. One end of the tool is hook-shaped and embedded with a tiny, single-edged blade. To cut the mat, simply slide the blade beneath a tiny portion of the knotted hair, with blunt edge against the skin. Do this only under good lighting conditions, so you can see and feel with your fingers that you are slicing through strands of hair—*not* the attached skin. Also, be careful not to poke the skin—yours or the cat's—with the tool's point. Do not use a sharp tool such as this on a cat that struggles and resists grooming, lest you injure the cat.

• To cut the knotted hair, gently lift the tool up and outward, toward yourself, as if ripping a hem out of a garment. Separate and cut small sections of the knot at a time until you can pull the tangle free. Obviously, you would not want to chop up a show cat's coat with these last-resort, cut-and-snip tactics. That's why it's easy to consider a few minutes of regular grooming at least two or three times a week as time well invested.

Trimming Claws

Besides grooming, toenail clipping is something every cat should get accustomed to at a young age. Like your fingernails, a cat's claws grow continuously and need to be clipped occasionally. Even with scratching posts available, an indoor cat's nails do not wear down as readily as those of an outdoor cat. Neglected, untrimmed claws can curve under and grow back into the paw pads, causing a painful swelling and abscess. Trim claws once a month or so and always prior to a cat show, if you intend to exhibit your pet. Regular trimming reduces the risk of injury to you and other family members, and helps prevent snags in your carpets and furnishings.

Cats retract their claws when not in use. To extend them for trimming, hold the paw with your thumb on top and fingers on the bottom and

gently squeeze. Before clipping, look closely at the nail and identify the *quick.* If the nail is white, the quick clearly shows up as a thin pink line running about three-quarters of the way down the nail toward the tip. To avoid cutting into the sensitive quick, trim the nail tip below the pink line. The quick contains nerves and blood vessels, but the nail tip below it does not. If you accidentally cut too high up into the pink quick, the cat will feel pain and the nail will bleed. If this happens, hold pressure over the wound with a cotton ball until the blood clots, or apply a shaving styptic.

With the cat held securely in your lap or placed on the countertop or table where you do your routine

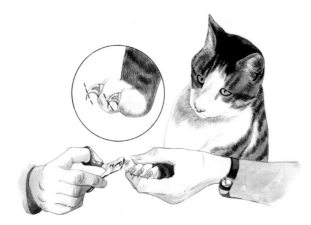

When trimming claws, clip only the white tips. Avoid cutting into the pink "quick," as this will cause pain and bleeding.

grooming, trim the claws on the front and hind feet. Start by clipping just two or three nails at a time, then add more as your cat gets accustomed to the idea. Use human or pet nail clippers for the job, then smooth the rough edges with an emery board or nail file. Don't forget the dew claw slightly higher up on each inside forepaw.

Bathing Your Cat

If you are going to show your cat, he will require a bath a day or two before the show to look his best in the ring. Otherwise, bathing your cat is necessary only if the coat becomes flea-infested, excessively oily, or otherwise soiled enough to require a thorough cleaning. Too many baths can rob your cat's coat of natural oils and dry the skin, so bathe only when your cat truly needs a thorough cleansing.

Shampoos: If you plan to exhibit your cat, you need to know that different coat types and colors demand different products to achieve that sparkle and ultra-clean appearance needed in the show ring. Every breeder and exhibitor has special preferences when it comes to shampoos and such, so start with the product your breeder or veterinarian recommends. Regardless of whether you're getting ready for a show or simply giving your cat a flea bath, here is one rule you should always follow when it comes to choosing shampoos and other products that touch your cat's coat and skin: *Use only products labeled as safe for use on cats.*

Bath supplies: In addition to shampoo, other supplies you'll need for the bath include:
• a comb
• cotton balls (for swabbing the ears)
• a blow dryer
• towels
• a washcloth
• a pitcher or shower spray attachment
• a source of clean, warm water for washing and rinsing.

The kitchen sink is usually the ideal place for the job, but if you must bathe the cat in a laundry tub, reserve a second tub of clean water for rinsing. For blow-drying the cat, you'll need a table or countertop with access to an electrical outlet. You'll probably also need a willing assistant, because many cat baths easily turn into two-person productions, especially if the feline is not fond of or used to the idea.

Preparations: To minimize the risk of injury to you and your assistant, trim the cat's claws first. Also before bathing, give the coat a thorough combing to remove mats or loose, dead hairs that could get tangled or set in wet fur.

If possible, close off the room where the bath will take place, so you won't have to chase a wet, soapy escapee through the house. Before putting the cat in the tub or sink, fill the basin partially with warm (not hot) water. A rubber bath mat in the bottom prevents slipping and makes the cat feel more secure by giving it something to grip.

How to Bathe a Cat

Have your assistant hold the cat down in the partially filled water basin with gentle pressure on the back and shoulders. Keep the cat's head above water and turned away from the direction of the spray or faucet. If the cat panics, talk to him reassuringly and gently hold him down by the scruff of the neck until he stops struggling. Be especially careful not to splash water in the cat's face or dunk his head under, as this will only increase his panic and create havoc for you and your assistant.

Wet the fur first with warm water, using the pitcher to dip and pour over the cat's back. If using a spray nozzle, keep the water pressure low to avoid frightening the cat. Don't spray water directly in the face. After wetting the fur sufficiently, apply shampoo and form a lather, starting at the neck and working back toward the tail. To lather the belly, have your assistant hold up the front legs. *Avoid getting soap near the face and eyes.* Use a damp washcloth or cotton balls moistened with warm water

to gently wet the head and wipe the face and eye areas clean.

The rinse cycle: Rinse thoroughly to remove all traces of shampoo. This is important because any residue left behind in the fur could make the coat look dull and greasy and cause itching and irritation. In some cases, the irritation may become so uncomfortable days later that the cat will actually scratch out portions of his fur, leaving behind ugly bald patches.

To rinse, use the sink spray nozzle or put the cat in a tub of clean, warm water, then dip and pour the water from the pitcher. When the fur feels squeaky clean, drain off the water and gently press out the excess by running your hands down the back, legs, and tail. Lift the cat out of the

tub or sink, being careful to support his rear end with one hand, and place him on a table or countertop for drying.

Blow-drying a cat: After bathing and rinsing, you must completely dry your cat before turning him loose in the house, especially in chilly weather. First, towel-dry the sopping fur as much as possible. Since towel-drying alone simply can't remove all of the moisture, follow up with a handheld or stand-mounted blow dryer.

Like bathing, many cats will learn to tolerate blow-drying if you exercise some sensitivity when introducing them to the idea. Use only the low settings, never the hottest setting. And never blow air directly in the cat's face.

Using a medium comb, gently comb the fur as you blow-dry, or separate the damp hair with your fingers, starting at the neck and working back toward the tail. Don't forget to dry the cat's underside. Have your assistant hold up the front legs for easier access to the belly and between the hind legs.

Cleaning the ears: Finally, use cotton balls to gently wipe away any dirt or wax visible just inside the earflaps, but *never* poke cotton swabs or other objects into the ear canal, as this could cause injury to the delicate inner ear structures. If the ears show an excessive amount of dirty, crumbly, brown wax inside, or if they exude a fruity odor, have your veterinarian check for ear mites or fungal infections.

Chapter Eight

Understanding Your Cat

Cat Language

Cats may not be able to speak our language, but that doesn't mean they can't communicate. They have an extensive vocabulary of mews and meows, and they communicate eloquently with one another using simple body language. When communicating their needs to humans, however, cats often combine vocal sounds with body language, perhaps recognizing that humans are not quite as adept as other cats at interpreting *feline-ese*. A typical exchange might involve leading the human caretaker to the cupboard, the refrigerator, or an empty food bowl and waiting patiently until dinner is served. If no food is forthcoming within a reasonable time, your cat likely will punctuate the exchange with plaintive, pitiful mews. Generally, the more urgent the request, the louder the meow.

Vocal Sounds

The cat's meow can express many moods and needs, depending on the intonation and intensity of the sound. For example, cats often use sweet-sounding little mews to greet their owners or acknowledge the sound of their own name. Bigger meows may be complaints or demands. A loud, throaty howl or a piercing yowl may mean your cat is in distress, such as being stuck up a tree or accidentally shut in a closet. Howling in an older cat, especially hearing-impaired ones, is also a distress signal that usually expresses mild, temporary disorientation related to declining cognitive functions natural to the aging process. Whatever the reason, the sound is often urgent-sounding enough to draw attention. Two other urgent vocal sounds, hissing and growling, are fear and warning indicators cats use to say "Back off" or "Leave me alone!" Of the two, growling is generally the more serious warning.

Queens in heat belt out a particularly annoying mating call to the neighborhood toms that is loud and persistent enough to rattle the nerves of the uninitiated. Simply referred to as calling, this distinctive and distracting sound is one of the hall-

marks of the feline estrus cycle (see page 166). Queens may reserve raucous vocals for sex, but after they become mothers, they chirp softly, in a most comforting and soothing way, when calling to their kittens.

Purring: This most universally recognized and beloved feline sound of all is also the most mysterious. Experts still puzzle over the exact mechanism that enables big cats and domestic cats alike to purr. Most scientists say the sound is probably produced by vibrations in the larynx, or voice box, as the cat breathes in and out. By whatever means, your cat can control and produce this soothing feline sound at will.

Why cats purr is really more mysterious than *how* they do it. There is a long-held belief that cats purr to express contentment, when they feel

happy, secure, warm, and well fed. But they've also been observed purring when nervous (at the veterinarian's office), upset, sick, hurt, or hungry. Interestingly, cats have even been known to purr when they are dying. Based on such observations, the generally accepted theory is that cats purr not only to express pleasure, but also to calm and comfort themselves when faced with an adverse situation.

Even kittens as young as two days old can purr, suggesting that the sound may have evolved as a special form of bonding between mother and offspring, a way to communicate and reassure that all is well in the nest. This theory seems plausible, given the fact that, for human caretakers, cuddling a purring cat can help relieve stress, promote a mutual sense of well-being, and strengthen the human/feline bond. Perhaps by purring in the presence of a trusted caretaker, cats are responding to us humans in the same way they would to a parent cat, letting us know that everything is okay.

Body Language

Being quiet, conservative creatures, cats tend to let their elegant bodies do most of the talking, resorting to vocal sounds when needed for emphasis or warning. A particular body stance, a simple turn of the tail, or the flick of an ear all can have specific meaning in cat language. For example, when your cat walks toward you with ears pricked forward and tail held high, with just the tip slightly bending forward, the animal is saying something similar to, "Hello, my friend. I'm sure glad to see you!"

When confronted by a stranger or an adversary, however, a timid or submissive cat crouches, lowers his ears, and drops his tail. A frightened or defensive cat can make himself appear as large as possible by arching his back and fluffing his fur out fully. An angry cat also crouches low, but his stance and tail action differs from that of the submissive cat. With ears flattened, muscles tense and ready to spring to action, the angry cat appears poised to attack. The flicking of his tail from side to side clearly signals a concise warning: "Back off!" If that posture fails to get the message across, a loud hiss or a low, drawn-out growl leaves no doubt that an attack is imminent.

Play-Hunt Postures

If you're fortunate enough to share your life with two or more cats at one time, you'll have the pleasure of watching them engage in mock battles and move through a series of attack postures, all purely for fun. Cats that know each other well often play and roughhouse in a seemingly ferocious manner, yet they generally keep their claws sheathed and seldom injure each other during these encounters. Kittens, especially, play this way, and by doing so, hone the skills they will use later in stalking and hunting prey.

Cat Fights

In a real confrontation, two cats may remain tense and still for several minutes, usually until one decides to make a strategic withdrawal. Being sensible creatures, cats generally

observe good territorial manners and are smart enough to avoid unnecessary *real* fighting, unless they're engaged in a serious dispute over dominance, territory, or mates.

When a real fight does develop, avoid getting in the middle of it physically, or you may get clawed or bitten. Instead, to break up a cat fight, clap your hands sharply and speak loudly and sternly. Or, make a loud, startling noise by banging on some appropriate object handy in the surrounding environment, such as pots or pans, for example. Do not throw anything directly *at* the cats.

Bonding

If you have more than one cat, you'll quickly learn to tell the difference between whether they are fighting or playing with each other. In time, you'll also begin to understand the meaning of each cat's personal repertoire of vocal sounds and body postures. In the process, you'll become quite adept at interpreting feline moods and emotions.

What's more, you may even start talking back to your cat, all the while swearing that your cat understands every word you say. In fact, the more you talk to your feline companion, the more vocal your cat likely will become when around you. Sharing this secret language is an integral part of the bonding process between cats and humans. People who never take the time to observe and learn these mannerisms miss out on an experience that can be extraordinarily satisfying.

Ideally, you will come to feel that no one else can understand or care for your cat as well as you do. Most important, you will be able to recognize, before anyone else, subtle changes in your cat's mood and behavior that can be important clues that all is not well as far as your cat's health is concerned.

The Cat's Primary Senses

Cats evolved to be nocturnal predators, creatures of the night on the prowl for prey animals that come out mostly under cover of darkness. Much of the mystery associated with felines is a direct result of their unique anatomy, which endows them with their special nighttime hunting prowess. Their mastery of the night has sparked awe, envy, and fear in the human soul throughout the ages—enough to, at various times in history, elevate the cat to the status of a god or damn the entire species as devils.

A cat possesses five known senses, all of which are far superior to ours. Understanding how your cat perceives his world through these highly developed senses helps explain many feline behaviors that appear incomprehensible otherwise.

Sight

As primarily nocturnal hunters, cats possess excellent night vision. Although they have poor color vision, cats can see much better in dim light

than humans; however, cats cannot see in total darkness. There must be some minimal light available for the feline eye to amplify. Their remarkable night vision stems from a special layer of cells behind the feline retina, called the *tapetum lucidum*, which makes a cat's eyes appear to glow in the dark. These specialized cells act like a mirror, reflecting all available light back onto the retina and giving the cat his exceptional ability to see well in low-light conditions.

The feline pupil can also dilate much wider than the human pupil. This allows the cat's eye to collect light more effectively in dim conditions. A cat that feels threatened, frightened, or defensive will dilate his pupils to see better over a wider area. Of course, the cat's pupil works the other way, too. On sunny days, the pupils constrict to vertical slits to block out bright light.

Well suited to hunting and night stalking, a cat's eyes are especially adept at detecting the slightest movements made by small prey animals. Many prey animals have evolved with the instinct to freeze in place and remain perfectly still when they detect the scent or presence of a nearby predator. A stalking cat hard at work will crouch patiently for long periods, staring at nothing, or so it seems, until the concealed or camouflaged prey finally reveals its whereabouts with barely a twitch in the grass.

Another special characteristic of the cat's eye is an opaque third eyelid, called the nictitating membrane, which helps protect and lubricate the eyeball. Although usually not visible under normal conditions (except occasionally when the cat is sleeping), the third eyelid may protrude from the eye's inside corner if the orb gets injured, irritated, or infected. In addition, this white, filmy membrane is sometimes more visible over the eyes with certain diseases and, therefore, warrants a veterinary examination if it persists beyond an occasional, sleepy blink.

Smell

Cats possess an acute sense of smell, far superior to a human's sense of smell, but not as keen as the dog's. Cats interpret the world around them largely through scent. As with dogs and other animals, cats use odors and the sense of smell to identify each other as well as objects in their territory. For example, when two cats meet on friendly terms, they typically engage in a ritual of sniffing each around about the head and anal areas, where scent glands exude a vast databank of personal information. Among cats, this behavior is the equivalent of the human handshake.

Your cat may greet you in a similar fashion, jumping in your lap, sniffing your face, then turning with tail in the air to present his rear end for examination. An appropriate human response would be a gentle back scratch at the base of the tail combined with loving pats, for in cat body language, your cat is actually exchanging a friendly "Hello!" Other behaviors such as licking, head butting, nuzzling, and rubbing are all

ways in which cats mingle their scent with their human or animal family members.

Jacobson's organ: Cats and many other mammals have a special scent mechanism, called the vomeronasal or Jacobson's organ, which enhances their sense of smell. This specialized scent organ adds a different dimension to animals' ability to detect and identify odors and is believed to give mammals an edge on finding mates by helping them sort out sex-related scent hormones called pheromones.

Located in the roof of the mouth behind the incisor teeth, this special organ actually allows cats to taste odor molecules. When using the Jacobson's organ, a cat curls his upper lip back and, with teeth bared and mouth partially agape, sniffs the air deeply through both nose and mouth. This grimace, often mistaken for a silent growl or a snarl, is called the flehmen response. Like many animals, cats sometimes display flehmen when examining urine and scent marks left by other animals and during territorial or mating rituals.

Taste

Specialized cells on your cat's tongue enable him to detect the chemical components of food as saliva dissolves them in the mouth. These taste buds send signals along nerve pathways to the brain, where taste identification actually takes place. The food with the greatest appeal to a carnivore's palate is, of course, meat. And being naturally evolved meat-eating predators, cats like their meals lukewarm, preferably as near the body temperature of most small prey mammals as possible—not hot, and certainly not cold, as in straight out of the refrigerator.

Pet food industry taste preference tests suggest that cats can distinguish between salty or sour foods, but they cannot taste simple sugars. According to the experts, this means that cats generally should not prefer sweet or sugary foods, although we've all heard owners' tales about cats that would kill for a chocolate chip cookie. But since many sweets are also high in fat, the cat with the sweet tooth is probably craving the yummy taste of the high-fat ingredients, and not the sugar.

Touch

Your cat's whiskers are highly sensitive tactile organs, so *never* clip them. There's a common saying that if a cat's whiskers can pass through a small opening, the cat knows the rest of his body can fit through and follow. This may be more fancy than fact—especially since obesity is such a common problem among today's house cats. It is a fact, however, that cats use their whiskers to sense and avoid objects in dim light and to detect vibrations and changes in their environment. Cats also use their whiskers to touch and gauge the size of prey caught in their paws.

Hearing

Few people are surprised to learn that cats can hear better than humans. Because their normal prey typically emits high-pitched sounds, cats' ears are tuned to frequencies well beyond the range of human hearing. Cats can also quickly learn to recognize the source and meaning of certain sounds; for example, chirping birds mean a possible meal is nearby. This associative ability extends from the hunting ground into the household, and after the first time or two, your cat likely will come running to the buzz of an electric can opener, the flip of a pop-top cat

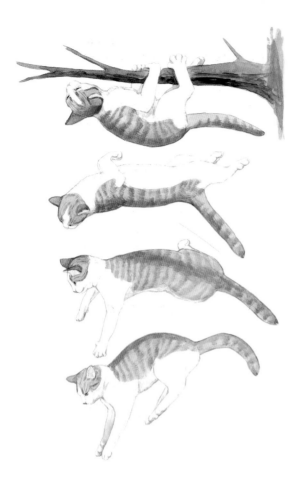

A balancing mechanism in the cat's inner ear enables the animal to right himself in mid-air during a fall.

rumbles its way over the rugs and floors. But try sneaking open the refrigerator door for a snack, and your cat will hightail it from the farthest end of the house to see what's cooking! Even from the soundest sleep, a cat can be instantly alert when he hears something of interest, swiveling his ears toward the source and peering intently in the direction of the sound.

Balance and the Righting Reflex

Besides their five primary senses, cats also possess an extraordinary sense of balance. If a cat rolls off a windowsill and falls in an upside-down position, a balance mechanism in the inner ear enables the cat to rotate his forequarters first, then the hindquarters, so that he automatically rights himself in midair and lands on all fours. This remarkable ability is known as the righting reflex. The cat's supple and flexible spine also contributes to his maneuverability in freefall. But even with these impressive assets, cats that fall from great heights can still sustain fractures and other serious injuries. In fact, veterinarians see so many of these types of injuries that they've classified them under a special name—*high rise syndrome,* as mentioned on page 46.

food can lid, or the opening of the refrigerator door. If you consistently call your cat by name at each feeding, he will quickly learn his name, and perhaps even come when called—if he feels so inclined.

Cats also appear to have the enviable ability to selectively tune out the cacophony of nerve-wracking noises in the normal household. They can sleep soundly in front of a blaring TV, snooze through a children's birthday party, and continue to catnap while the vacuum cleaner

Sleeping Habits

Insomnia is not a common problem among cats; they are well known for their excessive catnapping, often sleeping as much as 18 hours throughout the day. By evening, however, just about the time you're getting ready for bed, your cat's nocturnal hunting instincts may kick in, and he will be wide awake and ready for action. Your toes wriggling under the bed covers present the perfect prey to pounce upon, so beware! These nocturnal play sessions can be annoying to some people and probably contributed to the time-honored tradition of putting the cat out at night, no doubt so that a weary owner could get some sleep.

Fortunately, most domesticated cats seem to adapt readily to human diurnal timetables, adjusting easily to their owners' work and weekend schedules. In fact, many indoor house cats sleep soundly all night on their owners' beds, doubling as fail-safe alarm clocks as morning and the breakfast hour dawns. But some cats, particularly the more active breeds, will prowl the house during the night, at least for a few hours, exploring in the darkness and knocking a few toys about here and there, before finally settling down. If you're a sound sleeper, these nocturnal wanderings may not disturb you, but if they do, you may want to consider confining your cat to his own room at night. Or simply shut your bedroom door and leave the rest of the house to your cat to prowl at will. As with people, cats that get plenty of exercise generally sleep better. To exercise your cat and help him burn off excess energy, provide toys and play with him periodically (see Exercising Your Cat, page 103).

Hunting Habits

To observe your cat's hunting skills in action, use an interactive toy, such as a kitty fishing pole with sparklers or feathers attached to the end of the line. Throw out the line and slowly reel in your cat as he stalks the wriggling lure. Watch as your cat crouches and creeps forward silently, pupils wide and eyes fixed, looking for the slightest move that might mean the pretend "prey" is going to run. Muscles remain tensed and ready for instant pursuit. The tail twitches in anticipation. As

the cat prepares to pounce, he wriggles his rear end and treads quietly with the back legs, as if testing which foot will provide the better spring action. Before the feather flutters one last time, the cat springs upon it with claws extended, the front paws striking in deadly accuracy to pinion the prey. One well-placed death bite with the powerful canine teeth ends the struggle.

Even people who despise predation confess to being entertained and awed by the cat's fluid body coordination and rigid concentration during play-hunt sessions. The ancient

Egyptians worshipped the cat for his unequaled rodent control talents, yet modern-day cat enthusiasts often experience a paradoxical twinge of guilt when their cat's natural instincts bring down a fledgling sparrow. Even worse for some are the times when their outdoor cat brings home prey as a gift offering and deposits the corpse on the doorstep. Although disgusting to some people, this is normal instinctive behavior for cats. Experts say this ritual relates to the way cats perceive their human caretakers as family members. Mother cats bring dead or stunned prey to the nest and, by doing so, teach their kittens how to identify, hunt, and kill prey. Without this important behavior pattern, kittens probably would not easily learn to find food and fend for themselves.

So if your cat delivers a similar offering to your nest, don't be alarmed, and don't punish the cat for behaving like a cat. Simply praise your cat for his extraordinary generosity, then dispose of the gift quickly, so as not to prolong your cat's exposure to potential parasites or disease harbored by the unfortunate prey.

If predation disgusts you, prevent it by keeping your cat indoors. You'll do the wildlife in your yard a favor, and your cat certainly will remain healthier without contact with diseased or parasite-laden rodents or birds. Your cat will be safe from outdoor hazards and just as happy hunting indoors, preying on store-bought catnip mice.

Territorial Marking Behaviors

By nature, cats are highly territorial creatures and will readily notice any new objects or changes in their environment. Understandably, big changes, such as moving to a new house or apartment, can be extremely upsetting for some cats. Because some cats adjust more easily to changes in their environment than others, major moves or changes of any sort should always be handled in a sensitive and thoughtful manner, and always with your cat's welfare in mind. Understanding your cat's territorial habits can help you deal more effectively with problem behaviors that may arise as a result of environmental changes that have upset your cat.

Rubbing

Rubbing is one means by which cats mark objects in their environment and claim them as their territory. When rubbing against furniture and other objects, cats leave behind scent from glands around their faces, mouths, and tails. Humans can't smell the scent, but other cats can. The message means, "I was here first, and this territory is mine!" Whether indoors or outdoors, cats will routinely travel the boundaries of their territory to inspect and refresh these scent markers. Perhaps this helps them reaffirm that all is well in their environment.

One endearing habit many cats have—rubbing against their owners' legs in greeting—is much more than a mere gesture of affection. Like rubbing against objects, this, too, is a territorial marking behavior. Your cat views you as an integral part of his territory, and each time he rubs against you, he marks you with his scent, reaffirming ownership. In addition, the mingling of your smell on the cat's fur helps identify you as a member of his circle of friends. So in a sense, when your cat greets you by rubbing against your legs, he is really saying, "You belong in my territory. I own you!"

Spraying

Less endearing is the feline habit of spraying urine to mark territory. This territorial act can be distinguished from regular urine elimination by the cat's stance. When a cat eliminates, he squats on a flat surface, such as the ground, and urinates. When a cat sprays, he stands, rather than squats, with his back to a vertical surface and with his tail straight in the air. The tail quivers as the cat squirts urine to mark the wall, drapery, or furniture leg, and the liquid leaves telltale drip marks down the vertical surface.

Although males are more prone to this behavior, females sometimes do it to communicate their reproductive status, especially when in heat. Spaying and neutering—operations that eliminate the reproductive function in cats—tend to curb this undesirable behavior. But both sexes, whether whole or altered (commonly referred to as *fixed*), may occasion-

also fulfilling an instinctive need to keep his basic defense weaponry—his claws—sharp and trim. Similar to filing fingernails, the in-and-out action on wood, carpet, or rough fabric helps strip away the dead, outer layers of the claws.

Outdoor cats often sharpen their claws on the trunks of trees, leaving behind scent markers, undetectable to humans, in the process. For an indoor cat, this perfectly natural feline behavior can become an obvious problem if the animal singles out the sofa arm as a preferred scratching post. The scent left behind on your furniture, combined with the cat's apparent preference for the spot, continues to draw the cat back to the same site to claw until the sofa arm becomes a shredded mess. You cannot eliminate this instinctive need to claw, but you can modify it and redirect it by providing your indoor cat with an alternative scratching post, a suitable substitute for the tree trunk an outdoor cat uses.

Scratching posts: While it may take a little time and patience to persuade a cat to scratch at a scratching post, instead of your furniture or carpeting, doing so is the best way to avoid having your cat develop destructive clawing habits. For best results, start training early, when your cat is still a kitten, before an undesirable habit ever has a chance to start. Inappropriate clawing habits, once firmly established, can be difficult to break (see page 41 for a discussion on the types of scratching posts and their selection).

ally resort to spraying when engaged in a dispute with another cat over territory or dominance. For this reason, spraying is more likely to occur in multicat households, particularly if too many cats are housed in too small an area.

Clawing

When a cat scratches the arm of the couch, he is not misbehaving. Like spraying and rubbing, this action, too, is actually an instinctive territorial marking behavior. The cat is marking the scratched object with scent from glands in his paws and is

Regardless of the type of scratching post you choose, introduce your cat to it as soon as you bring the newcomer into your home.

1. Simply show the cat the post, move his paws in a scratching motion, and praise lavishly when he does what you want.

2. If necessary, rub some dried catnip on the post to entice your cat to play and climb on it.

3. If the cat decides to try out your furniture, scold verbally by saying *"No"* in a loud, sharp tone, or squirt jets of clean water from a water pistol to startle the cat without harming him.

4. Wait a few minutes, then carry the cat to his scratching post.

If clawing the furniture has already become an established habit, it will be harder to break, but not impossible. The recommended strategy is to make the inappropriate surface unattractive to the cat while, at the same time, offering a more appealing, acceptable substitute, such as a suitable scratching post. To discourage an undesirable scratching habit, cover the problem area temporarily with a loosely draped blanket, newspaper, wrapping paper, plastic bubble wrap, or sheets of aluminum foil. Then, as previously explained, consistently and patiently encourage the cat to use the acceptable substitute for his scratching needs.

In general, cats are easy to train and readily learn to respond to voice tones and commands. If you are consistent and persistent in your methods, your cat should soon learn to restrict his clawing to the designated area. When disciplining your cat, use your voice, but *never* strike the animal with your hand, with a folded newspaper, or with any other object. Such abusive action doesn't teach the cat anything and will only make your cat fearful and distrustful of humans.

Vinyl nail caps: Once a destructive clawing habit becomes firmly entrenched, and traditional efforts to redirect the habit have failed, one humane alternative for dealing with the problem is to glue vinyl nail caps onto a cat's freshly trimmed claws. These caps, which can be purchased from veterinarians, give the nails a soft, blunt tip and help prevent snags in carpets, furniture, and

drapes. The major drawback to this method is that the vinyl caps have to be reapplied every four to six weeks, as the nails grow. The application is simple, however, and owners can purchase take-home kits and learn to manicure their cats' nails themselves. Ask your veterinarian to demonstrate the product. Vinyl nail caps are not recommended for outdoor animals because they inhibit a cat's ability to climb.

Declawing: This is the least desirable alternative for dealing with destructive clawing and should be considered only as a last resort after other methods have failed. Banned in some countries, this controversial procedure is still performed in the United States by veterinarians who consider it a viable option over having to euthanize the cat or surrender him to an animal shelter for adoption.

The declawing procedure involves putting the cat under anesthesia and surgically amputating the claw tip and the last bone of the toe. Generally, only the front claws are removed, because the hind feet are not used for scratching furniture. While this procedure may offer a permanent solution to destructive clawing problems, it is not painless. After the operation, the cat suffers some pain and risk of infection as his mutilated paws heal.

Declawing has other drawbacks, too. The procedure renders a purebred cat ineligible for the show ring, because the major cat associations that sponsor shows disallow the practice for championship competition. In some associations, however, cats shown in the household pet division are not penalized for being declawed.

The procedure also clearly inhibits climbing and self-defense. With only the front claws removed, a cat still can use his rear claws to climb trees, but he can't climb as well as before. Therefore, cats allowed to roam freely outdoors should not be declawed and disadvantaged in this way.

Many people believe that robbing a cat of his natural defenses may harm the animal psychologically and make him more apt to bite in self-defense. Some owners report profound personality changes in their cats after the surgery. Others say their cats developed inappropriate toilet habits afterward, probably as a result of cat box litter irritating the tender incisions. Older cats seem to have more difficulty adjusting to life without claws than kittens.

Handling House-soiling

Destructive clawing and house-soiling are high on the list among the many reasons why cats end up at animal shelters, surrendered for adoption. Once a bad habit becomes well established, it can be difficult, although not impossible, to break. Some owners simply don't understand the motivating factors well enough to deal with them, or, lacking the patience to deal with the

problem, they give up too soon and give away the cat. Sadly, some of these problem behaviors probably could have been easily prevented from the outset, if only the owner had understood their significance as instinctive territorial behaviors.

Often, what people perceive as a behavior problem in the home is quite normal for cats living in the wild. Understanding what is normal behavior for cats under natural conditions is crucial to understanding how to deal with them when things go wrong under confined conditions. For example, cats, being naturally territorial, mark and defend areas where they spend most of their time. As discussed, clawing and spraying are two means of marking territory. Knowing what motivates a certain

Spiteful Cat?

Generally speaking, when a housebroken cat eliminates outside his litter box, the animal is either marking territory or displaying a preference for a particular spot, surface, or litter box filler. Contrary to popular belief, cats do not begin house-soiling out of spite. At least, that's what the behavior experts say, although many owners can reel off accounts of cats urinating on shoes or other belongings of people who've irritated or neglected them. Such accounts are largely a matter of interpretation; after all, who can truly say what goes on in a cat's mind?

behavior is the key to figuring out how to modify or correct it. This is especially true when it comes to house-soiling problems.

While spraying and litter box problems can occur in single-cat homes, they are more common in multicat households, particularly in overcrowded conditions. If you have more than one cat, you can help prevent elimination problems by providing each animal with his own litter box. Even then, a more aggressive cat may sometimes chase another away from the litter box, forcing the more submissive creature to eliminate in a corner or other inappropriate area of the house. If this happens, place the boxes far enough apart, in separate rooms or at opposite ends of the house, to give each cat a sense of privacy and individual territory.

Medical reasons: Whatever the cause, house-soiling is often symptomatic of emotional anxiety or physical discomfort. So whenever a cat begins eliminating in inappropriate places, consider urinary tract infections and other medical causes first (see page 118). Take your cat to the veterinarian for a checkup. If the cause turns out to be physical, prompt medical treatment usually can reverse the problem before it becomes an established habit. Always rule out disease or infection first, then pursue the behavioral or emotional approaches.

Spraying Versus Urinating

Determining whether a cat is spraying to mark territory or simply eliminating urine inappropriately can be difficult. Typically, the owner discovers the soiled area after the fact, seldom catching the cat in the act. But making the distinction, and understanding the difference, can help you decide how to effectively treat a house-soiling problem. A few simple clues may help.

• If the urine stain appears to start primarily on a vertical surface—a wall or furniture leg—and drip down, then, the cat is *spraying* to mark territory.

• If the urine is pooled on a flat, horizontal surface—the floor or the bedcovers—then, the cat is squatting to eliminate urine.

Ascertaining this difference is crucial because the factors that motivate each type of behavior are different. To effectively deal with either undesirable behavior, you must try to determine the factors causing or influencing the situation.

Here are some common motivating factors behind house-soiling problems:

Litter box location preference: A cat that squats and inappropriately urinates on the carpet or floor may simply be expressing a dislike for the location of his litter box or for the texture of the litter. Perhaps the box is in a high foot-traffic area or too close to a noisy furnace that frightens the cat when operating. Try moving the box to a quieter, more secluded part of the house, or if possible, place it at or near the site of the house-soiling accident. For whatever reason, the cat may prefer

that spot, and putting the box there may solve the problem.

Litter preference: If location doesn't seem to be a motivating factor, experiment with different types and textures of kitty litter. Some cats don't like litters treated with fancy perfumes and deodorizers, and will refuse to use them. Some cats prefer fine-grained litter that is like sand, while others are content with the larger, coarser clay granules.

Cleanliness: In many cases, failure to use the litter box occurs because cat and owner have different opinions about what constitutes a clean litter box. The owner may think cleaning the box once a week is enough; the cat may want it cleaned every day. Cats are fastidious creatures, and digging in dirty, damp litter must be disgusting to them — perhaps a lot like being forced to use an unflushed toilet. So,

if you're equally fastidious about removing the solid wastes daily and replacing soiled litter weekly, your cat likely will be more happily inclined to continue using the box without mishap.

Anxiety: Emotional causes of house-soiling are the most difficult to pinpoint. Sometimes the sight of outdoor cats or the introduction of a new pet or a new baby into the household can trigger territorial spraying. In this situation, veterinarians can prescribe drugs that may ease the cat's anxiety and help suppress spraying and aggressive behaviors.

Whatever the cause, punishing a cat for spraying or eliminating in inappropriate places is seldom effective and often makes matters worse. Rubbing your cat's nose in the mess will only make him fear you. Spanking the cat, then carrying it to the litter box may backfire and actually cause the animal to associate the abuse and fear with the litter box, an attitude that then becomes unnecessarily difficult to reverse. Rather than resort to punishment, identify and change the behavior by trial-and-error removal of any possible motivating factors, one by one, until you hit upon the right one, and the problem resolves itself. Whenever you feel the situation isn't improving, seek the advice of an expert—your veterinarian or even an animal behavior consultant.

Cleaning Up House-soiling Accidents

To deter the cat from using the same spot as a toilet again, clean up house-soiling accidents with enzymatic products that dissolve the odor. As long as the scent remains, it will continue to attract the cat back to the same place. In addition, it is important to clean up house-soiling accidents as quickly as possible, because the more times your cat uses the same place, the more ingrained the bad habit will become.

1. When cleaning up carpet stains, remember to clean the mat under the carpet, too, as the urine will have soaked through. If you can't lift the carpet to clean under it, use a syringe to inject solution under the rug, or soak the spot with an odor-neutralizing product. Several good odor neutralizing products can be purchased at veterinarians' offices or pet supply stores for cleaning up pet messes. A mixture of white vinegar and warm water also works fairly well, but avoid ammonia-based cleaners. Ammonia is a urine by-product and might attract the cat back to the spot.

2. After you thoroughly clean and deodorize the spot, make the surface less appealing to the cat by covering it temporarily with plastic, aluminum foil, sandpaper, window screen, or double-sided sticky tape. If possible, keep the cat completely away from the area for a while to break the habit.

3. For further reinforcement, use a water pistol or make a loud noise to startle the cat away from the area every time you see him near the spot.

4. For a different approach, try changing the significance of the area by placing food and water bowls there. Cats typically will not soil the area close to where they eat.

Social Behaviors in Multicat Households

Having more than one cat in the house can be rewarding to both cat and cat lover. The owner has an opportunity to compare and savor each feline's unique personality. The cats benefit by keeping each other company while the owner is away at work. Despite their aloof, solitary reputation, cats clearly enjoy each other's companionship and are highly social animals. In general, they seem able to adapt equally well to solitary or group living; however, as

previously noted, confining too many cats in a limited space can increase the incidence of behavior problems, particularly those attributed to territorial disputes. Signs of stress from overcrowding may include hiding, fighting, house-soiling, and excessive grooming, so naturally, you want to be careful not to acquire more cats than you can afford to feed or provide medical care for.

Fortunately, when living in social groups, cats tend to claim less territory, and boundaries become more flexible. Unlike dogs, which live in rigid pack structures, cats prefer fluid group hierarchies that tend to change over time. Individuals that bond as friends share space, sleep together, and groom each other. In general, the bigger your home, the fewer territorial problems your indoor cats are likely to develop, but if you have only so much room, expand the cats' available territory from floor to ceiling by installing vertical cat-climbing trees and carpeted kitty condos. These carpet-covered cat trees with tiered sleeping shelves make excellent scratching posts and provide ample exercise and climbing opportunities for indoor cats.

Cats, like children, often display jealousy over the attention another individual receives. Sometimes squabbles arise over something as simple as who gets to nap in that most revered spot—the owner's lap. So when you have more than one cat, take time to pet and play with each one. Respect their individual personalities and territorial needs. Provide each with his own food dish, litter box, toys, and bed. If mealtimes become too competitive, feed cats in separate rooms, as necessary. Your household will be much more tranquil, and you will cherish the insights you gain from sharing your living quarters and communicating with members of a different species.

Chapter Nine
How Cats Reproduce

Spaying and Neutering

Teach your children how proper health care, spaying, and neutering can reduce the suffering that more than eight million surplus pets endure each year. That's about how many animals wind up abused, neglected, and homeless in U.S. shelters every year. Most must be humanely destroyed because there simply aren't enough homes to go around for so many. The way to reduce this senseless waste of life is to end all indiscriminate breeding of both pedigreed and nonpedigreed animals by spaying and neutering pets and by never allowing intact cats to roam freely. Should you decide to allow your cat to bring kittens into the world, it is your responsibility to make sure that each kitten goes to a home where he will be wanted, loved, and cared for.

The Feline Facts of Life

Among breeders, an intact, breeding female cat is called a queen. An intact male is called a tom or stud. Ideally, a queen should not be bred until she is at least one year old, although her first heat cycle (estrus) may occur months earlier. Waiting a year allows the queen to achieve her full growth first, before essential nutrients must be diverted to nourish unborn kittens. A tom reaches sexual maturity between 9 and 14 months, and from then on, his hormones drive him relentlessly to search for mates and to defend his territory against intruding toms. His sex hormones trigger his instinctive urge to spray and mark his territory with strong-smelling urine, which is one reason why a breeding male in a cattery of purebreds typically is confined to a cage or spacious run. Neutering usually curbs this undesirable male trait, unless the habit has become well established.

The Queen's Heat Cycle

A queen comes into heat according to seasonal rhythms, usually in early spring, midsummer, and early fall. Feline reproductive cycles appear to be influenced by lengthening daylight hours, which explains why cats in the Northern Hemisphere have cycles opposite those in the southern half of the world. Most queens have heat cycles every two or three weeks during the breeding seasons; others cycle only once a month. Exceptions abound, however, and some cats living indoors in controlled, artificial lighting may cycle year-round.

A few queens have silent heats, but generally there's no mistaking when females come into season. The hallmark signs include increased restlessness and vocal calling. The queen may seem more affectionate toward her owners, rubbing against them and wanting to be petted. She may roll on the ground or pace from door to door. Take care to keep her in, for if she escapes outdoors, she may mate with more than one male and deliver a mixed litter of kittens having different fathers. The most obvious and nerve-wracking behavior at this stage is known as *calling*—the queen's persistent, drawn-out, throaty howl that advertises her availability to the neighborhood toms. In response to this calling, plus the high levels of sex pheromones the queen's body produces, yowling toms from near and far line up on the fence ready to prove their worthiness as mates.

The Mating Position

Also at this stage, the queen may crouch in the characteristic mating stance, called the estrus or lordotic posture. She will assume this posture, too, if you stroke her back near the base of the tail. With front end

pressed to the ground, and with back hollowed, she will raise her hindquarters, swish her tail to one side, and tread up and down with her hind feet, as if marching in place.

If the queen is bred and becomes pregnant, gestation normally lasts an average of

63 days. If mating does not take place, she enters a stage of sexual inactivity until her next cycle begins.

The Sex Act

When all goes according to nature's plan, the queen rolls provocatively for her suitor and assumes the mating stance, inviting the tom to mount her. The tom seizes her by the scruff of the neck and proceeds to pedal with his hind legs. The brief coupling ends with a howl and a hiss from the queen as the tom withdraws. Often, she turns to swat him with her paw. The two go off by themselves momentarily to groom or to watch the other, but soon they will rejoin and repeat the mating sequence many more times.

Induced Ovulation

Female cats are unusual in that they, unlike most other mammals, do not ovulate spontaneously during their cycles. Instead, they are *induced ovulators*, meaning that the sex act must occur, usually repeatedly, to induce the release of eggs from the ovaries. To accomplish this, the male's penis is ridged with tiny spines or barbs that scrape the inside of the queen's vagina during copulation. This physical stimulation apparently sends a message along nerve pathways to areas in the brain that release a luteinizing hormone, a chemical that prompts ovulation.

Signs of Pregnancy

About three weeks after conception, the queen's nipples redden, called pinking up. Her attitude may become more maternal and affectionate. Her appetite may increase, and she will gradually put on a few extra pounds. Proper nutrition is vital for the queen's health and for the developing fetuses. A veterinarian can recommend a cat food specially formulated for reproductive needs.

Cats, like people, can suffer from morning sickness due to hormonal changes. The queen may vomit occasionally during her third or fourth week, but the problem usually lasts only a few days and requires no veterinary treatment unless it becomes severe. Report any other signs of illness to your veterinarian immediately.

The queen's abdomen becomes noticeably swollen in about a month. Resist the temptation to palpate the kittens inside, as they or the distended uterus can be injured easily by inappropriate handling. Leave this inspection to your veterinarian. For the same reason, do not allow children to pick up the queen during her pregnancy.

Preparing for Birth

The average length of pregnancy in the cat is 63 days. After breeding your queen, make a note on your calendar, a week or so before the expected delivery date, to have a veterinarian examine her to ensure that all is well.

The entire time the queen is pregnant, and later while she is nursing, feed her a high-protein, high-quality feline growth and reproduction formula. Her protein needs will increase dramatically during the second half of her pregnancy, so follow your veterinarian's feeding guidelines. Also, unless directed by your veterinarian, avoid giving medications to your queen or using flea preparations on her while she is pregnant and nursing. Keep her indoors, especially during the last few weeks of pregnancy.

A Kitten Nest

To prepare for the birth, make a kittening box for the queen to nest

in. This can be a large cardboard or wooden box with a cut-out doorway and removable lid. Line the box bottom with old, clean towels, and place it in a warm, secluded, draft-free area, away from other pets and distracting noises. As the due date draws near, the queen's natural instincts will instruct her to rummage in closets and hideaways, looking for a suitable nesting site. When you notice this activity, show her the box, and she likely will figure out its intended purpose. If she accepts the nest, place her feeding bowls and a litter box nearby.

Birthing Supplies

Some supplies to assemble before the delivery include:
• a heating pad or hot water bottle for warming the nest
• an eyedropper or small ear syringe for clearing airways
• an antiseptic solution for treating the umbilical stumps
• scissors for cutting cords
• a hemostat for clamping cords or unwaxed dental floss (or thick cotton thread) for tying cords.

Delivering Kittens

At labor's onset, the queen may pant, cry loudly, and appear restless. She may go to the litter box and appear to strain, perhaps confusing her contractions with the urge to eliminate. If this is her first litter, the queen may appear confused and distressed about the unusual sensations she feels. Talk to her reassuringly and minimize noise and

distractions around her. If she seems upset by your hovering presence, observe her progress from a respectful distance, but do not leave her alone until all kittens are safely delivered. If complications arise, she will need your help immediately.

As labor progresses, the queen may crouch or lie on her side. She may sit up frequently to lick her vulva. When the contractions become more forceful, birth is imminent. You may see some straw-colored fluid discharge as the water sac around the first kitten ruptures, lubricating its passage through the birth canal. From here on, things move rapidly, with kittens arriving about 15 to 30 minutes apart in most cases, although this can vary.

Presentation: About half of all kittens arrive head first; the other half emerge hind feet and tail end first. This tail-first presentation is no cause for alarm unless you see the kitten's bottom but no feet. This means the hind legs are folded toward the head and is a true breech presentation that could complicate delivery. Call your veterinarian immediately.

Amniotic sac: Each kitten emerges either completely or partially enclosed in a grayish, semitransparent bubble, called the amniotic sac or placental membrane. Most experienced queens will instinctively strip this sac away, sever the umbilical cords, and forcefully lick each kitten clean to stimulate its breathing and circulation. But a queen having her first litter may not know what to do, so be prepared to assist by gently pinching the sac open and wiping mucus from the kitten's nose and mouth so it can breathe.

Umbilical cord: If the kitten is breathing and wriggling, there's no rush to cut the umbilical cord. Blood passes through the cord to the kitten from the placenta. When this blood flow stops, the cord constricts. If the queen gets busy delivering another kitten and neglects to chew through the cord, simply clamp or tie it 1 or 2 inches (2.5 to 5.1 cm) from the kitten's navel. Then cut the cord just beyond the clamp or knot on the placental side. Dip or swab the stump with antiseptic solution. Always soak your ties and instruments in antiseptic solution before use. If using ties, trim ends short, so that only a minimal amount of string remains around the umbilical stump.

Reviving a kitten: If the kitten isn't breathing, you'll have to cut the cord immediately so you can attempt to revive the kitten.

• Rub the kitten briskly with a soft cloth and clear the secretions from its face. Suck excess fluids from the airway with an eyedropper or a small ear syringe.

• If that doesn't work, hold the kitten securely in both hands, firmly support the head so it doesn't flop, and sling the kitten upside down several times in a wide arc to force fluids from its respiratory passages.

• If the kitten still doesn't respond, blow tiny, gentle puffs of air into its mouth and nose and swing again.

• Once revived, warm the kitten by placing him next to a hot water bottle or on a heating pad.

• Put him back with the mother when she finishes delivering.

Placentas: Throughout the delivery, count placentas carefully. There should be one delivered with or just after each kitten. A retained placenta can cause a serious post-natal infection. Also, never tug on the umbilical cord before the placenta is expelled

completely. Doing so may tear the queen's uterus and cause life-threatening complications. Don't be alarmed if the queen eats the placentas; this is her instinctive way of cleaning the nest so that predators won't be attracted by the birth odors. As soon as possible after delivery, remove the soiled towels from the kittening box and replace with clean, fresh bedding.

Trouble Signs During Birth

In most cases, the entire litter arrives within two to six hours. On rare occasions, a queen delivers half of her litter, goes out of labor to rest, then delivers the other half many

hours or even a day later. If the queen appears at ease and is contentedly tending to her kittens, there may be no need to worry. However, it's easy to confuse this condition with a more serious one, called *uterine inertia*, in which the contractions fade and the queen appears too tired to carry on. Because a veterinarian can best judge the situation, seek medical advice if labor stops for more than two hours between kittens, especially if the queen seems weak, listless, restless, or anxious.

If the queen bears down for an hour without producing a kitten, or if she partially delivers one and is obviously in distress, call a veterinarian or transport her to a clinic immediately. Do not wait until she is too exhausted to deliver normally.

After the birth, it's always a good idea to have your veterinarian examine the queen to make sure there are no retained placentas or other abnormalities. Also, be on the lookout for persistent bleeding afterward, or any foul-smelling discharge from the vagina, which may indicate internal tears or infections.

Kitten Development

Healthy kittens begin suckling just minutes after birth. It's important that they nurse right away so they can ingest disease-fighting antibodies contained in the mother's first milk, called the colostrum. Born with eyes and ears closed, each kitten selects his own nipple and seeks out the same teat each time to nurse.

If the kittens cry a lot and seem fretful, they may not be getting enough milk. Depending upon the problem, a veterinarian may be able to correct it by giving the queen a hormone injection to stimulate her milk flow.

After each meal, the mother licks the kittens' genitals to make them urinate and defecate. Should you ever find yourself faced with the grueling task of hand-raising and bottle-feeding kittens, you, too, will have to play Mom and stimulate elimination by massaging their tiny bottoms with a warm, damp washcloth.

A healthy newborn weighs an average 3 or 4 ounces (about 100 g) and should begin gaining weight rapidly in a couple of days. If one kitten is a runt or appears to be gaining less weight than the others, have a veterinarian examine him.

A day or two after birth, the umbilical stumps dry and fall off the newborns. In about 10 days, the kittens' eyes begin to open. At first, all kittens' eyes are blue, changing to their adult shade at about 12 weeks of age. By 15 to 20 days old, kittens start crawling. Soon afterward, they begin to stand and toddle.

Socialization: From age three weeks on, handle and play with the kittens daily. Experts say that kittens socialized to humans at an early age grow up to be better-adjusted, people-oriented pets. At one month, kittens begin to play with each other, engaging in mock chase and combat games intended to hone their hunting skills. Also by this time, they

can control their own elimination, and litter box training can begin. Raising kittens in a confined area keeps them safe, and also helps them become trained faster.

Weaning: After four to six weeks, kittens can experiment with soft, solid foods. You can begin weaning with a commercial kitten milk replacer, such as KMR (available through veterinarians and pet stores). To let kittens try some solid food, supplement mother's milk with meat varieties of bottled baby food mixed with canned kitten milk replacer. A half-and-half mixture of canned, evaporated milk and water will also do, but avoid homogenized cow's milk, as it can cause diarrhea. If refrigerated, warm milk to room temperature before serving. Test it with your finger to make sure it's not too hot.

Starting with a saucer of warm milk introduces the kittens to the idea of eating a familiar food out of a dish, but don't expect their table manners to be polished and pristine the first time. They will almost cer-

tainly climb in with all four feet, so be prepared to mimic mama cat's rough tongue by gently wiping them clean with a warm, damp washcloth afterward. As the kittens become accustomed to eating out of a dish, start adding small amounts of canned commercial kitten food to this milk formula.

Gradually increase the amount of solid food, then gradually decrease the milk formula until the changeover is complete. As you begin decreasing the milk formula, remember to place clean, fresh water in a shallow bowl for the kittens to drink. Also, once the kittens become accustomed to eating moist, solid foods, it's time to start mixing in some dry commercial kitten food. At first, soften the dry food with warm water or milk formula to make it easier to chew. Taste preferences are established at an early age, so if you want your kitten to like eating dry food when he grows up, it's important to start getting him accustomed to the tastes and textures while he's young. By the time kittens are old enough to be fully weaned, they should be able to chew dry food.

By about six or eight weeks, kittens should, in most cases, be fully weaned and ready to leave their mother, although many breeders of purebred cats will not release their kittens to new homes until 12 to 16 weeks of age. The reason for this is twofold: Certain breeds mature more slowly than others; also, some breeders prefer that their kittens have a complete set of vaccinations

before letting them go to a strange, new environment.

Basic Feline Genetics

Parents pass on their individual characteristics and qualities to the next generation of kittens via the genetic code contained in coiled strands called chromosomes. All body cells, except sperm and eggs, contain these chromosomes arranged in pairs. Cats have 19 pairs per cell, or 38 total. The sex cells, however, contain 19 single, unpaired chromosomes. When egg and sperm cells unite to form a new individual, the chromosomes pair up again to total 38, bringing half of the genetic code from the father and half from the mother.

Genes

Chromosomes are made of a molecular material, called DNA (deoxyribonucleic acid), which carries the genetic code for how a kitten will look and behave. Bits of this code, such as eye color and coat length, are stored in smaller heredity units called *genes.* Genes are often called the building blocks of life because thousands of them, lined up along the chromosome strand, spell out the genetic blueprint for the entire animal. Most traits in the animal are produced by the complex organization and dynamic interaction of numerous genes. In some cases, a single gene can influence more than one trait.

Occasionally, a random change in the genetic blueprint causes a mutation in the individual that inherits the altered gene. Some mutations are bad, but others may benefit an individual by enabling him to adapt and survive better in his environment.

Because chromosomes are paired, genes for specific traits also are paired, one from each parent. This random sharing and pairing of genetic material from both parents is what allows species members to enjoy such remarkable diversity and individuality.

Paired genes are also called *alleles*, and the gene that expresses its coded trait is said to be dominant. The other is recessive. Recessive genes can express their coded traits only when paired. For example, the gene for a short hair coat is dominant, while the gene that produces the Persian cat's luxurious long coat is recessive. Long- and shorthaired genetics is discussed further on page 8.

Color inheritance: Some colors and markings are produced by recessive genes, while others, generally the more common ones, are produced by dominant genes. Some coat colors are paired with other traits, as with the blue eyes that accompany the pointed patterns in breeds such as the Siamese. Similarly, the association of deafness with blue-eyed white cats is well known, although not as well understood.

Gender: The sex chromosomes determine whether the cat will be a male or a female. All females have two sex chromosomes labeled XX; males have two sex chromosomes labeled XY. When these chromosomes pair up, one from each parent, to create a new individual, an X from the mother combined with an X from the father produces a female (XX) kitten. A male (XY) kitten results if the mother's X chromosome pairs with the Y from the father. Because only males possess the Y chromosome, the father determines each kitten's sex. Besides determining gender, sex chromosomes also can carry genes for other traits, and such traits are said to be sex-linked. Certain colors and patterns, such as red (also called orange), tortoiseshell, blue-cream, and calico are sex-linked traits carried on the X chromosome.

Professional Breeding Strategies

Professional breeders attempt to concentrate a purebred cat's good qualities by breeding it to related cats that likely carry the same desirable genes. Unfortunately, *inbreeding* mother to son, father to daughter, and so on, concentrates any bad qualities present in the family bloodline along with the good. *Linebreeding,* or mating distant relatives, achieves similar results, but often with fewer detrimental effects. Frequent outcrossing to separate bloodlines of the same breed helps keep the gene pool healthy and vigorous.

When permitted by the cat fancy's governing bodies, *crossbreeding*, or mating cats of different breeds, can be used to increase the gene pool or to create new breeds and colors. For example, the Himalayan is a cross between a Persian and a Siamese. While such matings can certainly occur accidentally or randomly under unsupervised conditions, the offspring cannot be registered. Therefore, this particular breeding strategy is generally only purposely employed by knowledgeable breeders who are trying to create a new breed of cat or new varieties and colors. In certain circumstances, the governing bodies of the cat fancy may permit crossbreeding to increase the gene pool within a particular breed.

Registering a Purebred Litter

After a litter of purebred kittens is born, a professional breeder sends a form and fee to the cat-registering association(s) with the breed type, birth date, sire and dam's registration numbers, and color and sex of each kitten. The registry sends back a litter registration, plus individual registration forms to use for registering each kitten in the litter.

Registering an Individual Kitten

Depending on the terms of the sale, the breeder gives one individual registration slip to each person who buys a kitten. If the buyer agrees to spay or neuter the kitten, the seller may choose to withhold the registration slip and send it later, after receiving proof from a veterinarian that the operation has been performed.

On the individual registration form, the breeder completes the section for the kitten's sex, breed, eye color, coat color, and so forth. If the breeder has a cattery name, it will be printed on the line where the buyer writes in the name chosen for the kitten. The cattery name becomes part of your cat's registered name, for example, Cattery XYZ's Miss Fluffy.

Most associations' forms direct the buyer to select two or three names, in case someone else already has used the first-choice name. When the registry receives the form with the appropriate fee, it will verify the pedigree information, approve a name selection, and then send the buyer an official owner's certificate.

Chapter Ten
Showing Your Cat

Most people who own a beloved cat find themselves drawn to a cat show sooner or later. Besides being the best place to meet dedicated breeders and fellow feline lovers, cat shows are enjoyable and educational. You can learn a lot about cat care simply by observing the way exhibitors groom and ready their entries for the judging ring. You can also learn a lot about the different breeds by listening to judges' comments as they examine each cat. Large shows also attract numerous vendors that display and sell cat-motif gifts, toys, grooming aids, and accessories. Even if you never intend to show your cat, attending a few cat shows will be rewarding adventures. To learn about upcoming shows in or near your area, check listings in cat fanciers' magazines. The cat-registering associations also can provide information about affiliated cat shows and clubs in your area (refer to Useful Addresses and Literature, page 188).

Breed Standards

A cat show is not simply a beauty contest, although grooming and appearance are extremely important. Every pedigreed cat competing in a show is judged according to how well he meets the written standard for his particular breed. A breed standard is a written blueprint describing the ideal conformation and coloring of animals representing that breed. The standard describes in detail how the head, body, coat, and color should appear in the ideal specimen. To successfully show cats, you must be familiar with the breed standard accepted by the association(s) sponsoring the shows in which you exhibit.

The breed standard also dictates the goals of a professional breeding program. For use in their breeding programs, conscientious breeders try to select cats that most closely fit the standard or that possess enough of the desired qualities outlined in the standard to promise outstanding offspring. Ideally, their aim is to breed the best to the best, whenever possible.

Breed standards can vary among the different cat associations, as well as from country to country. Practices for accepting new colors and varieties can vary widely, too, and some associations or countries may

recognize colors not currently accepted elsewhere.

From time to time, breed standards may be revised or rewritten by formal committees that convene periodically to amend and update them. This is due to the fact that selective breeding sometimes results in new colors or varieties that need to be added to the standard after meeting certain criteria for acceptance. Breed standards may also change on occasion because the favored look of a breed evolves and changes over time.

So, if you're planning to enter a show, be sure to acquaint yourself with the breed standard and rules of the association that is sponsoring that show. Contact the appropriate association(s) and request the most current information (see Useful Addresses and Literature, page 188).

How a Cat Show Is Organized

Although cat shows originated in Great Britain, those held there today are quite different from the ones in the United States. In Great Britain, judges go from cage to cage examining cats; during some judging, they even ask owners to leave the show hall. In the United States, however, judging takes place on judging tables set up in one area of the show hall in full view of all spectators and exhibitors attending. Behind each judging table is a row of cages, where cats entered in the same category are called to await judging. This setup of tables and cages is called a judging ring.

A single exhibition may have four or more judging rings set up, each operating as a separate competition

and presided over by a different judge. Sometimes, separate clubs present back-to-back shows consisting of eight to ten rings over a two-day weekend. Cats can compete in all rings for which they are eligible. In the ring, the judge removes each cat from his cage, places him on the judging table in view of the audience and thoroughly examines him. After evaluating all cats in the ring, the judge awards first- second- and third-place ribbons to the winners.

A certain number of wins qualifies a cat as a champion or grand champion. The highest awards at a show include Best of Breed and the most coveted prize, Best in Show. Cats that win in the championship or premiership (for altered cats) finals earn points based on the number of cats defeated at the show. These points count toward regional and national titles. To understand the ribbons, points, and awards system more fully, consult the rules booklet prepared by the cat association sponsoring the show, as this may vary from one association to another.

Types of Shows and Classes

All-breed and Specialty Shows

If a show is billed as an *all-breed* show, all purebred cats, regardless of their type, compete against each other. *Specialty* shows, on the other hand, may be restricted to specific breeds or breed groups. Most commonly, specialty shows are restricted to the longhaired or shorthaired breeds. Depending on the association sponsoring the show, various divisions and classes exist for eligible pedigreed cats, altered cats, kittens, household pets, and new or experimental breeds and colors. Typically, pedigreed kittens between four and eight (or in some associations, ten) months of age can compete in classes with other kittens of their breed.

Generally, unaltered, adult pedigreed cats begin their show careers competing in *open* classes against others of their breed, sex, and color. After achieving a specified number of wins, they become champions and can compete against other champions for the coveted title of grand champion. Many associations award additional titles beyond these.

New Breeds and Colors

Practices for accepting and showing new or experimental breeds, colors, and varieties differ among the associations, but most allow such newcomers to be exhibited in non-championship classes, after they've been accepted for registration. Depending on the association sponsoring the show, these classes may be labeled as Provisional, Miscellaneous, NBC (New Breeds and Colors), or AOV (Any Other Variety) classes.

In general, new breeds are exhibited first in noncompetitive, miscellaneous, NBC, or AOV classes before being granted prechampionship, or provisional breed, status. Cats in provisional breed competition are judged according to a provisional standard, but once their new breed gains full recognition, they become eligible for championship classes.

Alter Classes

These classes, called *premiership* classes in the CFA, allow spayed and neutered pedigreed cats to compete against other altered cats of the same breed. Altered cats are judged according to the same standards as whole or intact cats, but instead of qualifying as a champion or grand champion, they earn comparable titles of *premier* or *grand premier* in the CFA. Many novice exhibitors prefer to show in alter classes, because acquiring and owning a show-alter cat affords an opportunity to compete on equal footing with breeders who've been in the business for years. Yet, having a show-alter relieves newcomers to the cat fancy of the extra commitment involved in keeping a breeding animal. So, if you have a purebred cat that you want to show, but you have no interest in breeding him, showing in premier or alter classes may be the best route to go.

The Household Pet Category

Many people are surprised to learn that most major cat shows have classes for mixed-breed or nonpedigreed cats. Clubs and associations that sponsor the classes do so to promote the human/animal bond and to elevate the status of the common alley cat. Spectators at cat shows may admire the purebreds, but they readily recognize the household pets as being most similar to Fluffy at home. Show organizers hope that people will be encouraged to take better care of their pet cats when they see how beautifully presented and valued they are at a show.

Called the household pet or HHP category, competition is open to nonpedigreed cats at least four months old. Household pets older than eight months must be spayed or neutered to compete. CFA and CFF do not permit declawed cats to be shown, but the other associations do not exclude or penalize HHPs for having had their claws removed. To further celebrate the value of all pets, regardless of their origins or misfortunes, TICA and ACFA allow HHPs with physical handicaps, such as a missing leg or eye. TICA also has a general written standard for household pets, whereas not all of the associations do.

HHPs can be of any size, color, or hair length. Depending upon the association sponsoring the show, HHPs may be shown against other cats of the same color, or they may all be judged together. Unlike purebreds, HHPs are not judged according to a formal breed standard. Instead, they are judged on more general and subjective terms for their overall condition, beauty, personality, and an elusive quality called show presence. The more friendly, poised, or playful they are in the show ring, the better their chances of winning.

Most HHPs are mixed breeds of unknown ancestry, but some are pet-quality purebreds that do not meet their breed's written standard. Although policies vary from one registry to another, some cat-registering associations permit a purebred cat to be shown as a household pet, as

long as the owner surrenders the papers or does not register the cat as a purebred.

Awards and titles: Like purebreds, HHPs also compete for awards and titles, although the names differ from one association to another. In TICA, for example, household pets strive to win their Masters, with the most coveted honor being Supreme Grand Master. In the AACE, HHPs progress in rank from Regal, to Imperial, to Superior Household Pet.

In some associations, points scored at each show accumulate toward year-end awards. The Happy Household Pet Cat Club also gives its members national, regional, and state awards every year based on a cat's performance throughout the show season. If you're going to show frequently, the tracking of year-end awards is one reason why you would want to register your household pet with the associations sponsoring the shows you compete in. TICA, ACFA, CFF, AACE, UFO, and TCA all maintain registries for nonpedigreed cats.

Getting Started in Cat Shows

If you own a purebred cat that you want to show, the breeder you purchased the animal from may be willing to be your mentor and help you get started in cat shows. When asked, most serious and reputable

What to Bring to the Show

- a small litter box, just in case
- your grooming equipment
- a grooming table (a sturdy TV tray or plastic patio table will serve the same purpose)
- a cat carrier
- a cat bed
- food and water bowls
- your cat's favorite food
- any other accessories to make your cat feel comfortable.

It's also a good idea to take a gallon (3.8 L) or two of water from home, or bottled water, because different drinking water can sometimes bring on a bout of diarrhea.

breeders will encourage novices because your wins in the show ring can reflect favorably on their bloodlines and cattery name. Another good way to become involved in showing cats is to join a cat club in your area that is affiliated with one of the cat-registering associations. Many of these clubs may organize and put on annual shows in their area.

Once you've located a show in or near your area, entering it is simply a matter of filling out the proper entry forms and paying an entry fee. Contact the show's entry clerk for an entry form and ask about the rules. If you're going to show a nonpedigreed cat, make sure the show includes a household pet division. Also, if your cat is declawed, make sure that he will be allowed to compete in this particular show. You don't want to be disqualified on the day of the show simply because you didn't ask about the rules in advance.

Benching

Your benching assignment is the cage where your cat will stay when he is not being judged in one of the rings. Cages for a single cat are small—usually about 2 feet wide by 2 feet high by 2 feet deep (61 × 61 × 61 cm). But for a little extra money, you may have the option of requesting a double cage on the entry form you submit. Usually, there is a place on the entry form where you can request to be benched next to someone you know. If your mentor, or someone you know who is an experienced exhibitor will be exhibiting at the show, ask to be placed next to that person.

Show Preparation and Supplies

After you return your forms and pay the appropriate entry fees, all you have to do is to get your cat ready and presentable for the show date. On the day of the show, you will need to bring some spray disinfectant to wipe down your cat's cage, as well as fabric, towels, or show curtains to line the inside and bottom of the cage. Covering the cage gives your cat a little privacy amid the show hall noise and shields him from seeing the other cats in adjacent cages. This also adds an element of fun, because many shows have contests for the best-decorated cage.

Generally, the show committee provides a chair at each cage, cat litter, and sometimes disposable litter boxes.

Of course, you will have completed most of your cat's grooming at home, having bathed him a day or two before the show and having made sure that your cat has no sign of fleas. Only touchups should be required at the show, but be prepared and take all your grooming supplies with you, including a battery-powered blow dryer, just in case your cat makes a major mess of his fur in transit.

The Day of the Show

When the big day arrives, your cat must be flea-free and disease-free to enter the show hall. In some countries, such as Great Britain, many shows are *vetted*, meaning that a veterinarian screens each cat before he or she is allowed inside the show hall. Although U.S. shows do not require vetting, inoculations must be up to date. The show flyer the entry clerk sends you will state whether you must bring proof of current vaccinations for rabies or other diseases.

After you check in at the door on the day of the show, and get your cat settled in his assigned cage, read the catalog schedule to determine when your cat will be judged. Also, note the number for your entry in the catalog, as this is how your cat will be called to the ring. Give yourself at least an hour before the show's actual starting time to check in, set up, and get your things organized. Then, once the show starts, keep your ear tuned to the public address system. When you hear your cat's number called, carry your cat to the appropriate judging ring. Your number will be posted on top of one of the cages in the ring. Place your cat in the correct cage, then take a seat in the audience to quietly watch the judging.

Judging: The judge will examine each cat in turn on the table and hang ribbons on the winners' cages at the end of the class. When the judging is over, the clerk will ask the exhibitors to remove their cats from the ring. Collect your cat and ribbons, if any, and return to your benching cage to await your call to the next ring. Depending on how well your cat does, he may be called back for finals, when the top contestants in a given category are presented.

Traveling to Shows with Your Cat

Travel by Car

Although your first cat show may be within easy driving distance of your home, traveling to the show may be a stressful ordeal for your cat. Some cats enjoy riding in a car, but most do not. Some even get carsick. Most people seldom take their cats for a ride in the car, except when they're going to visit the veterinarian. But if you're going to show your cat, he will experience a lot less stress if you take the time to get him accustomed to traveling in a car while he's still a kitten. Take your cat for short drives around the block every few days, gradually increasing the time spent in the car.

Safety in transit: For safety and control, keep your cat in a pet carrier while traveling. This practice not only minimizes escape opportunities, but also prevents a frightened or exploring cat from getting under the gas and brake pedals or otherwise interfering with the driver's ability to control the car. Cats and dogs have been known to accidentally free themselves from the confines of a car by stepping on and activating the button pads that operate electric car windows. Confining your cat to a carrier prevents this opportunity for escape, lessens the risk of injury during an accident, and reduces the likelihood of escape through a broken window or an open door during an accident. To prevent the carrier from being tossed about during a mishap in transit, strap it securely in place with the car seat belt.

For extremely long drives, set a litter box in the floor of the car so you can let you cat out of his carrier for rest stops. When you do so, stop the car and do not open the car doors or windows while your cat is out of his carrier. If your cat is leash-trained, secure him on a harness and leash whenever he comes out of the carrier. Stay with your cat at all times. Because of the risk of heatstroke, *never* leave your cat unattended in a parked car, especially on warm days, (see first aid information for heatstroke, page 134).

Travel by Air

If you find it necessary to travel to a show by air, make sure your cat carrier conforms to the airline's regulations. Many pet-travel accidents are a result of poorly constructed carriers. A standard shipping carrier should be made of metal, sturdy wood, fiberglass, or rigid plastic. One entire end must be open for ventilation and covered with metal bars or heavy wire. The remaining sides should have ventilation slots, and all ventilation slots or holes should be protected by protruding rims to prevent obstruction by other baggage. The door latch and joints of the container must be escape-proof and impervious to biting and clawing. The container must be clearly labeled with *Live Animal* and *This End Up* and tagged with the cat and owner's names and address, plus any feeding instructions.

Some airlines allow pets in the passenger cabin as carry-on luggage, but they must remain in a special-size carrier that fits under the seat. Other airlines allow animals to be transported only in the cargo hold, and some offer special expedited delivery service for animals. Most require a health certificate issued by a veterinarian.

Although aircraft cargo holds are pressurized and temperature-controlled during flight, onboard hazards can arise during delays on the ground, before takeoff and after landing, when the plane's compartments are not air-pressurized. During that time, temperatures inside the cargo hold can fluctuate rapidly. Careful planning can help minimize these dangers when transporting an animal by air. Whenever possible, book a nonstop flight, avoid holiday or weekend travel, and avoid flying during excessively hot or cold periods. Also, when you board the plane, make sure the airline pilot knows that there is an animal in the cargo hold.

Warning

Although tranquilizers may relieve some of your cat's travel anxiety, drugs also may make an animal more susceptible to temperature changes and breathing problems. Because tranquilizers can have unpredictable side effects in some animals at high altitudes, use them only under the advice and guidance of a veterinarian.

Hotel: If you're staying overnight, the show flyer should recommend hotels that allow pets. If the show is going to be held at a hotel's convention center, special arrangements or accommodations may be made for the exhibitors and their cats. If not, ask in advance about the pet policy at the place where you plan to stay, and don't forget to take a litter box for use in the hotel room. If you must leave your cat alone in the hotel room for brief periods, put the animal in his carrier. When you leave the room, hang out the Do Not Disturb sign. You don't want housekeeping personnel to enter while you're dining out and let your precious cat accidentally slip out the door.

Responsible Pet Ownership

Regardless of whether you want a cat to show or simply to treasure as your companion, remember that your conscientiousness as a cat owner will inevitably be noticed by others. In this way, you have an opportunity to demonstrate to others by your own caring actions how to properly tend to a feline companion. Many cat owners take this responsibility seriously and strive to become the best-educated pet owners they can be. They visit shows, attend pet-care seminars, promote spaying and neutering, participate in clubs, and read books and magazines about cats. Some even volunteer to serve and support their local humane shelters, helping to improve the plight and existence of all cats, not just purebred ones.

Such an attitude is admirable, because the cat or kitten you acquire and raise to adulthood represents a significant financial and emotional investment on your part. The more strongly you communicate the value of this investment to others, the more likely you are to instill a similar appreciation in others about cats in general. In this way, you can make a difference by enlightening others and by simply helping to raise their awareness of what it really means to be a responsible and caring pet owner.

Useful Addresses and Literature

North American Cat Registries

American Cat Fanciers Association (ACFA)
P.O. Box 1949
Nixa, MO 65714-1949
(417) 725-1530
Web page: *www.acfacat.com*

Canadian Cat Association (CCA)
5045 Orbitor Drive
Building 12, Suite 102
Mississauga, ON L4W 4Y4
(905) 232-3481
Web page: *www.cca-afc.com*

Cat Fanciers' Association (CFA)
1805 Atlantic Avenue
P.O. Box 1005
Manasquan, NJ 08736-0805
(732) 528-9797
Web page: *www.cfainc.org*

Cat Fanciers' Federation (CFF)
(937) 787-9009
Web page: *www.cffinc.org*

National Cat Fanciers Association (NCFA)
10215 West Mount Morris Road
Flushing, MI 48433-9281
(810) 659-9517
Web page:
  www.nationalcatfanciers.com

The International Cat Association (TICA)
P.O. Box 2684
Harlingen, TX 78551
(956) 428-8046
Web page: *www.tica.org/*

United Feline Organization (UFO)
5603 16th Street W
Bradenton, FL 34207
(941) 753-8637
Web page:
  www.unitedfelineorganization.net

Nutrition-related Organizations

Association of American Feed
 Control Officials, Inc. (AAFCO)
c/o Georgia Department of
 Agriculture
Agriculture Building, Capitol Square
Atlanta, GA 30334
Web page: *www.aafco.org*

Pet Food Institute
2025 M Street, NW, Suite 800
Washington, DC 20036
(202) 367-1120
Web page:
 www.petfoodinstitute.org

WALTHAM Centre For Pet Nutrition
Waltham-on-the-Wolds
Melton Mowbray
Leicestershire, England
Web page: *www.waltham.com*

Noteworthy Organizations

ASPCA Animal Poison Control
 Center
1717 South Philo Road, Suite #36
Urbana, IL 61802
(888) 426-4435
Note: A fee may apply
Web page: *www.aspca.org/
 pet-care/poison-control/*

The Humane Society of the
 United States
2100 L Street, NW
Washington, DC 20037
(301) 258-8276
Web page:
 www.humanesociety.org

American Society for the Prevention
 of Cruelty to Animals (ASPCA)
424 East 92nd Street
New York, NY 10128-6804
(212) 876-7700
Web page: *www.aspca.org/*

Cornell Feline Health Center
Cornell University College of
 Veterinary Medicine
Hungerford Hill Road
Ithaca, NY 14853
(607) 253-3414
Web page:
 www.vet.cornell.edu/FHC/

The Delta Society
875 124th Avenue NE, Suite 101
Bellevue, WA 98005
(425) 679-5500
Web page: *www.deltasociety.org/*

Food and Drug Administration's
 Center for Veterinary Medicine
 (FDA-CVM)
10903 New Hampshire Avenue
Silver Spring, MD 20993-0002
(888) INFO-FDA (1-888-463-6332)
Web page: *www.fda.gov/
 animalveterinary/default.htm*

Happy Household Pet Cat Club
14508 Chester Avenue
Saratoga, CA 95070
Web page: *http://hhpcc.org/*

Morris Animal Foundation
10200 East Girard Avenue B430
Denver, CO 80231
(800) 243-2345
Web page: *www.morrisanimal
 foundation.org/*

Cat Publications
CATS Magazine, Primedia Special
 Interests
260 Madison Avenue, 8th Floor
New York, NY 10016
www.catsmag.com

Cat Fancy
P.O. Box 6050
Mission Viejo, CA 92690
(714) 855-8822
www.petchannel.com

Catnip (newsletter)
Tufts University School of
   Veterinary Medicine
(800) 829-5116
www.tuftscatnip.com

CatWatch (newsletter)
Cornell University College of
   Veterinary Medicine
Subscriptions:
P.O. Box 420235
Palm Coast, FL 32142-0235
(800) 829-8893
www.catwatchnewsletter.com

About.com: Cats
An online newsletter
http://cats.about.com

Books

Association of American Feed Control Officials, Inc. (AAFCO) Official Publication (published annually). For order form or purchasing information, visit *www.aafco.org*.

Carlson, Delbert G., D.V.M., and James M. Giffin, M.D. *Cat Owner's Home Veterinary Handbook.* New York: Howell Book House, 1995.

Burger, I. H., ed. *The Waltham Book of Companion Animal Nutrition.* Oxford, England: Pergamon Press, 1995.

Davis, Karen Leigh. *Fat Cat, Finicky Cat: A Pet Owner's Guide to Pet Food and Feline Nutrition.* Hauppauge, New York: Barron's Educational Series, Inc., 1997.

____. *Mixed Breed Cats: A Complete Pet Owner's Manual.* Hauppauge, New York: Barron's Educational Series, Inc., 1999.

____. *The Everyting Cat Book*, 2nd ed. Avon, Massachusetts: Adams Media, 2007.

Helgren, J. Anne. *Encyclopedia of Cat Breeds: A Complete Guide to the Domestic Cats of North America.* Hauppauge, New York: Barron's Educational Series, Inc., 1997.

Hotchner, Tracie. *The Cat Bible.* New York: Gotham Books, 2006.

Moore, Arden. *The Cat Behavior Answer Book.* North Adams, MA: Storey Publishing, 2007.

Robinson, Roy. *Genetics for Cat Breeders.* 3rd ed. Oxford, England: Pergamon Press, 1991.

Robinson, I., ed. *The Waltham Book of Human-Animal Interaction: Benefits and Responsibilities of Pet Ownership.* Oxford, England: Pergamon Press, 1995.

Siegal, Mordecai, and Cornell University. *The Cornell Book of Cats.* New York: Villard Books, 1997.

Thorne, C., ed. *The Waltham Book of Dog and Cat Behaviour.* Oxford, England: Pergamon Press, 1992.

Wills, Josephine M. and Simpson, Kenneth W., eds. *The Waltham Book of Clinical Nutrition of the Dog and Cat.* Oxford, England: Pergamon Press, 1994.

Whiteley, H. Ellen, D.V.M. *Understanding and Training Your Cat or Kitten.* New York: Crown Trade Paperbacks, 1994.

Index

Acid-base balance, 72
Alcohol, 93
Allergy, 24–25, 127–128
Amino acids, 64
Amniotic sac, 170
Antioxidants, 70, 74
Anxiety, 163–164
Appetite loss, 81, 107
Appliances, 47–48
Artificial colors, 75–76

Babies, 55
Balance, 154
Bathing, 45, 144–146
Beds, 41
Birds, 53, 55
Birth, 168–169, 171–172
Black Death, 2–3
Bleeding, 134
Blow-drying, 146
Body language, 149
Bonding, 150
Bones, 93
Books, 191
Bot fly larvae, 121–122
Bowel disease, 66
Breakable items, 47
Breeder
  quality cats, 33
  questions from the, 32
  questions to ask, 31–32
  strategies, 176–177
Breed(s), 6–12
  mutations, 12–13
Breed standard, 178–179
Brushing, 142

Calcium, 71, 90
Carbohydrates, 65
Carnivorous cat, 59–60
Catnip, 44
Cat(s)
  in America, 3
  care, 56–57
  domestication, 1–2
  fancy, 4–6

fights, 149–150
food, 60–63
from gods to devils, 2
language, 147–150
origin of, 1–3
proofing home, 46–48
registry, 33–34, 177,
  188
supplies, 36–46
today, 3
trees, carpeted, 42
walks, 105
Cat show, 6
  day of, 184–185
  getting started, 182–184
  organization of, 179–180
  traveling to, 185–187
  types of show, 180–182
Children, 54–56
Chocolate, 51, 92–93
Choking, 136
Choosing a cat
  adult vs. kitten?, 18–19
  animal shelter, 25–27
  cat vs. kitten?, 34–35
  costs, 22
  housing concerns, 23
  indoor vs. outdoor cat?,
    16–17
  kittens, 29
  male vs. female?, 19
  medical history, 35
  one vs. two cats?, 18
  pet allergies, 24–25
  pet store, 29–30
  purebred, 30–34
  purebred vs. mixed-
    breed?, 17–18
  registration, 33–34
  sale agreement, 33
  stray cat, 27–28, 27–29
  things don't work out,
    25
  time away from home,
    23–24
  your age and health, 25

your future plans, 22–23
your lifestyle, 22–25
your will, 25
Christmas tree, 51
Clawing, 158
Claw trimming, 143–144
Coat stripping, 141–142
Collar, 58
Colors and patterns,
  13–15
Combing, 141
Cosmetics, 47
Costs, 22
Countertops, 48

Death, 136–137
Declawing, 160
Dental care, 128–130
Dishes, 36–38
Dog food, 88–89
Dogs, 52–53
Drapery cords, 47
Drugs, 93
Dry-weight analysis, 84

Ears, 146, 153–154
Eating, competitive, 97
Electric cords, 46–47
Euthanasia, 136–137
Exercise, 103–105
External parasites,
  112–127
Eyes, 150–152

Facts of life, 166–168
Fat, 66–67
Feeding
  active cats, moderately,
    79
  finicky eater, 87
  guidelines, 85–86
  kittens, 76–78
  older cats, 79–81
  over, 97
  pregnant cats, 78–79
  what not to feed, 88–93

Feline diseases, 28,
  112–119
FeLV vaccination, 111
Ferrets, 53–54
Fiber, 65–66
Fibrosarcomas, 111
Finicky eater, 87
Fireplaces, 47
First aid, 133–136
Fish, 54
Fitness
  age and food, 98
  body condition, 94
  obesity, 38, 66, 94–99
FIV infection, 28
Flavoring agents, 76
Flea(s), 122–123
  allergy, 128
  comb, 141
Flukes, 121
Food
  bulk-feeding, 102–103
  canned, 61
  cat, 60–63
  commercial cat, 60–63
  diet, fish, 91–92
  diet, homemade, 86–87
  diet, therapeutic, 63
  diet, too-rich, 98–99
  dietary changes, 81–82
  dieting, successful,
    102
  dieting dangers, 102
  dry, 37, 60–61
  labels, 82–85
  low-fat food, 101
  popular vs. premium
    brands, 62
  premium brands, 62–63
  safe diet, 101–103
  semimoist, 61–62
  supermarket brands, 62
  weight-loss diet,
    100–101
Frostbite, 134–135
Fur, 138

Garbage, 93
Genetics, 175–176
Giardia, 119, 121
Grooming
    benefits of, 138–139
    introduction to, 140–143
    supplies, 44–45
    tools, 140

Hair balls, 132–133
Handling cats, 28
Handwashing, 55
Health
    feline diseases,
        112–113
    illness signs, 106–108
    preventive care,
        108–113
Hearing, 153–154
Heartworms, 119–120
Heat cycle, 166–167
Heatstroke, 134–135
Hobby supplies, 47
Holiday hazards, 50–52
Hookworms, 119–120
Hotels, 187
Household chemicals,
    47
House-soiling, 160–164
Hunting habits, 155–156

Jacobson's organ, 152

Kitten(s)
    choosing a cat, 29
    delivering, 169–171
    development, 172–174
    feeding, 76–78
    milk, 88
    nest, 168–169
    registering, 177, 188
    reviving, 171
    socialization, 173–174
    weaning, 174–175

Language, 147–150
Leash training, 105
Lice, 123, 126
Litter box, 39–41,
    162–163, 165

habit changes, 107–108
    training, 40
Lungworms, 119, 121

Magnesium, 70–73
Mating position, 167
Mat removal, 143–144
Medication, 130–132
Medicines, 47
Microchips, 58
Milk, 88
Mineral(s), 70–72
    supplements, 89–90
Mites, 123, 126
Multicat household,
    164–165
Mutations, 12–13

Neuter/spay, 20–22, 98,
    166
Newborns, 29
Nutrients, 63–72
Nutrition
    life-cycle, 76–81
    organizations, 189

Obesity, 38, 66, 94–99
Ovulation, induced,
    168

Parasites
    control, 124–125
    external, 112–127
    internal, 119–122
Pet(s)
    carrier, 38, 134, 185
    identification, 57–58
    other, 52–54
    quality cats, 33
Phosphorus, 71, 90
Picking up cat, 54–55
Placentas, 171
Plants, hazardous, 49–50
Play-hunt postures,
    149
Playmate, 104–105
Playtime, 104
Poison control, 189
Poisoning, 135
Pregnancy signs, 168

Pregnant cats, 78–79
Preservatives, 74–76
Proofing home, 46–48
Protein, 67–68
Publications, 190–191
Pulse, 127
Purebred, 17–18, 30–34
Purring, 148–149

Rabies, 115–116
Raw food, 91
Registration, 33–34, 177,
    188
Reproduction, 166–169
Reproductive organs,
    20–22
Reptiles, 54
Resources, 188–191
Responsible pet
    ownership, 187
Ringworm, 123, 126–127
Roundworm, 91, 119–120
Rubbing, 157

Scratches, 56
Scratching posts, 41–43,
    158–159
Screening, flimsy, 47
Self-feeders, 37–38
Self-waterers, 38
Sex act, 167–168
Shedding, seasonal,
    139
Show-quality cats, 33
Sight, 150–152
Sleeping habits, 155
Small mammals, 53
Smell, 152
Social behaviors,
    164–165
Socialization, 173–174
Spay/neuter, 20–22, 98,
    166
Spiteful cat, 161–162
Spraying, 157–158,
    162–164
Stoves, 48
String and yarn, 43–44
Struvite stones, 73–74
Sump pumps, 47

Tags, 58
Tapeworms, 119–120
Taste, 152–153
Tattoo, 58
Teeth brushing,
    129–130
Temperature, 127
Territorial marking,
    157–160
Ticks, 123, 125–126
Tobacco, 93
Toilet lids, 47
Touch, 153
Toxoplasmosis, 55–56
Toys, 43, 104, 165
Toys, hazardous, 47
Training
    litter box, 40
Tranquilizers, 186
Trash cans, 48
Travel, 23–24, 185–186
Treats, 97–98
Tuna, canned, 92

Umbilical cord,
    170–171
Urinary tract health,
    72–74
Urinating, 162–164

Vaccinations, 28,
    108–111
Vaccine reactions, 111
Vermin bait, 47
Veterinarian, 106
Vinyl nail caps, 159–160
Vital signs, 127
Vitamins, 68–70, 74,
    91–92
Vitamin supplements,
    89–90
Vocal signs, 147–149

Walks, 105
Water, 87–88
Weaning, 174–175
Weight, 79–81, 85, 94
Window perch, 45–46

Yard hazards, 48–50